Lasting hope through Jesus' cries from the cross

Steve Chick

Illustrated by Meg Leigh

kevin
mayhew

kevin
mayhew

First Published in Great Britain in 2019
by Kevin Mayhew Ltd, Buxhall, Stowmarket, Suffolk IP14 3BW
Tel: +44 (0) 1449 737978 Fax: +44 (0) 1449 737834
E-mail: info@kevinmayhew.com

www.kevinmayhew.com

© Copyright 2019 Steve Chick.

The right of Steve Chick to be identified as the author of this work has been asserted by him in accordance with the Copyright, Designs and Patents Act 1988.

The publishers wish to thank all those who have given their permission to reproduce copyright material in this publication.

Every effort has been made to trace the owners of copyright material and we hope that no copyright has been infringed. Pardon is sought and apology made if the contrary be the case, and a correction will be made in any reprint of this book.

All rights reserved. No part of this publication may be reproduced, stored in a retrieval system, or transmitted, in any form or by any means, electronic, mechanical, photocopying, recording, or otherwise, without the prior written permission of the publisher.

All Scripture quotations, unless otherwise indicated, are taken from the Holy Bible, New International Version®, NIV®. Copyright ©1973, 1978, 1984, 2011 by Biblica, Inc.™ Used by permission of Zondervan. All rights reserved worldwide. www.zondervan.com The "NIV" and "New International Version" are trademarks registered in the United States Patent and Trademark Office by Biblica, Inc.™

VOICE FROM THE HILLS by Philip Greenslade Copyright ©CWR 2008 Used with permission.
THE PROBLEM OF PAIN by C. S. Lewis copyright @ C. S. Lewis Pte Ltd. 1940
THE SILVER CHAIR by C. S. Lewis copyright @ C. S. Lewis Pte Ltd. 1953
Extracts reprinted by permission

9 8 7 6 5 4 3 2 1 0

ISBN 978 1 84867 624 4
Catalogue No. 1501602

Cover design by Rob Mortonson
Edited by Virginia Rounding
Typeset by Angela Selfe

Printed and bound in Great Britain

Yet now he has reconciled you to himself **through** the death of Christ in his physical body. As a result, he has brought you into his own presence, and you are holy and blameless as you stand before him without a single fault.

Colossians 1:22 [New Living Translation]

CONTENTS

About the author   7

Why *'Through'*?   8

Preface	Famous Last Words	11
Chapter 1	The Big Picture	19
Chapter 2	Just Forgiveness	33
Chapter 3	First Man Home	51
Chapter 4	A New Community	65
Chapter 5	Victory Through Defeat	81
Chapter 6	Dying for a Drink	95
Chapter 7	Mission Accomplished	111
Chapter 8	The Hands of God	125
Chapter 9	The Sign of Four	139
Chapter 10	The Shadow of the Cross	153
Appendix	40 Days Through Lent	161

ABOUT THE AUTHOR

Steve Chick is 55 years old and has had the joy of being married to Annie for the last 29 years. They have two grown-up children, Meg and Joe, who are themselves now married and living away from home.

For the last eight years Steve has been the Lead Elder at Hope Church, Winchester. The Church is part of the Commission family of churches in the UK (part of Newfrontiers worldwide). Previously he was part of the senior leadership team of Kings Community Church in Southampton for 15 years.

Steve is a passionate follower of 'The Saints' (Southampton FC) and the Welsh Rugby team and so is used to coping with unrealistic dreams and crushing disappointment!

His desire to write this book has been birthed out of personal heartache and the pastoral experience from over 20 years of church life.

WHY 'THROUGH'?

This book may be short but it has been a while in the making. My desire to write about Jesus' seven cries from the cross has had a lengthy germination period. Much of what you will read is loosely based around material prepared for preaching at Hope Church on Good Friday mornings over a period of several years.

The idea for the title of the book was inspired by a painting of a scene from World War I, by the artist Francis Martin. The more I thought about it, the more appropriate the title seemed. Through Jesus' words we find answers to the questions of life and death. Through Jesus' death we find relationship with the God who created us. Through Jesus' subsequent resurrection from the dead we find hope that goes beyond the grave. Through Jesus we are saved.

My long-standing captivation with the cross of Christ is rooted in two things. First of all, a conviction that what the Bible says is true and relevant to each and every one of us. Secondly, my own life-changing encounter with Jesus. I had genuinely put my trust in him when I was nine or ten years old. However, by the time I reached my early twenties I was like the prodigal son that Jesus so vividly talks about in Luke chapter 15. I had squandered my inheritance of faith and was lost, far from home. No one else was to blame. Even though I still believed in Jesus, Christianity had become a veneer that masked my inner turmoil.

All my efforts to put things right with God failed miserably. It was then that God unexpectedly and mercifully broke into my life. I finally began to understand that it was not about what I did, but rather about what Jesus had already done on my behalf. His death and subsequent resurrection was the key. Henceforth, everything changed in my relationship with God. I will be forever grateful for the cross.

For the last 18 years I have had the privilege of being a pastor in a local church, during which time I have experienced at first hand the brevity of life. These experiences are part of the driving force behind why I have taken time out to write. I want others to know that what Jesus said and accomplished on the cross provides the answers to the questions that death poses. My prayer for all of you reading this book is that you will come to a deeper appreciation of Jesus Christ.

I have tried to write in a way that is easily understandable for all. God willing, that will be your experience. Wherever appropriate, I have used personal stories and illustrations which I trust will enable you to apply what Jesus is saying to your own life. My hope is that, with the help of the Holy Spirit, you will find food for your soul.

Many years ago a lecturer at Southampton University drew an analogy between my written work and a soup. Occasionally something 'meaty' floated to the surface but for the most part it was bland and insipid. The worst thing about his brutal assessment was that it was true! Sadly, I could never get that excited writing about geography...

Jesus, however, inspires my love and devotion. As I have been writing about him I have sensed the nearness of God and the encouragement of the Holy Spirit. This gives me confidence that, if you take some time to meditate on what you read, it will do your soul good.

This book is not an attempt to be the first or indeed the last word on this matter, rather just a contribution. Many people, much more able than I, have written on this awe-inspiring and pivotal moment of human history.

I'd love to say a big thank you to Annie, my family and everyone at Hope Church Winchester who have made this book possible – especially Anne Wan, Dave House and David Howard. Last but not least, it has been a joy for me to work alongside my daughter Meg who has illustrated the book.

This process has strengthened my faith and stirred me to love Christ more. May this book do the same for you.

Much grace
Steve

PREFACE

FAMOUS LAST WORDS

Death, not space, is the final frontier. We are all certain of having to make that voyage whether we like it or not. What was for me just a vague shadow somewhere out there on the horizon has come more sharply into focus as the years have relentlessly rolled by. The pity, with something so significant for each and every one of us, is that we only get one go at it!

As I get older, death has become less of a laughing matter. The irreverent Monty-Pythonesque attitude portrayed in the film *The Meaning of Life* was once mildly amusing. The Grim Reaper knocks at the front door and requests the company of the guests at the dinner party. Their time is clearly up. He receives a typically understated British response: 'That's put a bit of a dampener on the evening.' In truth, there is nothing to smile about.

Having been at the bedside of many people as they face death and having been present at too many funerals, the occasional moments of black humour simply serve to mask the pain and sadness of losing a loved one. Death is a thief and a murderer. It cuts no deals and there is no stay of execution for good behaviour.

It provokes questions that we are not sure we want the answers to . . . 'Will we see them again?' and more personally, 'What will happen to me when I die?' The easiest way to deal with such questions, and the route taken by most, is not to think about it until it is too late. Many of us would secretly agree with the film director Woody Allen's acerbic conclusion that, even though he isn't afraid to die, he'd rather not be there when it happens.[1] The closer we get to the top of the escalator of life the fewer people there are in front of us. This brings with it a growing sobriety and increasingly desperate attempts to avoid reaching the top. Who can give us answers to the questions death poses?

Spending time with people who know they are dying reveals a range of emotions. At one end of the spectrum are fear, anger, denial, stoicism and sadness, and at the other love, tenderness and kindness. Our final minutes and last words remain long in the memory of those left behind, so what we say and how we say it can leave an enduring legacy. Yet, because no one knows when the curtain will eventually fall, there is often no meaningful last exchange and usually what is said is not worth repeating. The conclusion of the film *Braveheart* where William Wallace, having been hanged and drawn, takes his last breath and cries out 'Freedom!' inspires us with hope. Yet it very rarely finishes like this (I rather think, if it had happened like the film portrays, which of course it didn't, the last word to have come out of his mouth was more likely to have been 'Aaargh'). More often than not, at such moments, it is hopelessness that spills out of the human heart. This does not make for enjoyable listening. Who would want the job of transcribing the harrowing last words from the cockpit of a crashing plane from the recording on the black box? Not me.

I have had too many personal encounters with unexpected bereavements. In October 1990 my 55-year-old father was killed in a car crash. He was travelling the couple of miles home one Thursday afternoon. As the traffic lights at the junction

---

1. *Without Feathers*, 1975.

changed to green and he pulled away, his car was hit side-on. The driver of the other car was a student, new to the area. He had been unable to stop at the red light and gambled on 'flying' the lights. The point of impact was on the driver's door. My father would have been unconscious immediately. I still vividly remember the phone call that fateful day with my mum telling me he was unlikely to pull through the emergency operation. My wife, Annie, drove the 170 miles to Swansea whilst all I could do was pray that my dad would live. We arrived minutes after the life support machine had been switched off. There was no happy ending and no last goodbye.

On the other hand, I have also had the privilege of spending time with people who, knowing they were facing the inevitability of death, exuded indefatigable hope to the last. Each had a rock-solid confidence that this was not the end and that there was hope beyond the grave. Were they fooling themselves and simply denying reality? Were they sticking their heads in the sand like the proverbial ostrich? Or did they know something we all need to know? Let me tell you about just one of them.

Adrian had been one of my closest friends since we were teenagers. Our love of football and punk rock music was part of the cement that bonded a friendship that would last a quarter of a century. We were best men at each other's weddings. Our first children, both girls, were born within two months of each other. It was inevitable they would be friends (something that is still ongoing). Despite living at opposite ends of the country we regularly met up and planned holidays of a lifetime together. In May 2005 our two families, by now eight of us, went to Florida. As we were going, Adrian was unwell, having been diagnosed with a stomach ulcer. Despite his discomfort, his doctor gave him permission to travel and said he should be fine. Within a few days of arriving it became clear that wasn't the case. Eventually, the travel company flew him, his wife and their two children back to the UK. Within a week of getting home he was diagnosed with terminal stomach cancer. I saw him as much as I could over the next five months. I prayed, like many others, for his recovery. In the end there was no miracle. Indelibly etched in my memory is our last conversation. It was a Sunday lunchtime after church. The phone rang. Adrian wanted to talk to me. He asked me to be an executor of his will, to which I said, 'We can chat about it when I see you next Thursday.' I will always remember his reply . . . 'I won't be here.' Somehow he knew he was going to die in the next few days. Our last words were of our love for each other, our friendship over many years and a deep confidence that, because of our faith in God, we would see each other again. I still have that confidence. There is a day coming when I will take the same journey and I will see him again.

Hope beyond the grave. Virtually everyone wants it to be true. Some believe it is true – I do. Yet there is no empirical or scientific evidence to confirm what we hope for. So what is my confidence based on? A book. Actually, a collection of 66 books, and a person. The book is the Bible and the person is Jesus.

Written by a multitude of authors over centuries, the Bible conveys the consistent message that there is hope beyond the grave. In what is believed to be the earliest written book of the Bible (although the date of writing is unknown), Job deals with the difficult questions of suffering and pain. Job, the main character and the writer, calls out in his suffering: 'If a man dies, will he live again?'[2] This echoes the cry of every

---

2. Job 14:14.

human heart throughout every generation. Job's question was unanswered for hundreds of years until one day at a graveside just outside Jerusalem. His question was answered by Jesus, who was at the tomb of a close friend. Lazarus had just died and everyone, including Jesus, was grieving. Suddenly, Jesus made an extraordinary statement: 'I am the resurrection and the life. He who believes in me will live, even though he dies; and whoever lives and believes in me will never die.'[3] And to prove that what he had just said was true, he raised Lazarus from the dead.

Millions of people over the centuries since Jesus' great declaration have put their faith in what he said. Are his words true? Why should we believe him, especially when, bizarrely, not many months after making this promise he himself died? Actually, he was crucified on a Roman cross.

We can have no doubt how Jesus lived and no doubt how he died. His life and death are historically well documented by extra-biblical sources. However, the Bible makes the startling claim that having died, Jesus, God's Son, came back to life three days later. The writer of the book of Hebrews in the New Testament explains to us why this had to happen: 'Because God's children are human beings – made of flesh and blood – Jesus also became flesh and blood by being born in human form. For only as a human being could he die, and only by dying could he break the power of the devil, who had the power of death. Only in this way could he deliver those who have lived all their lives as slaves to the fear of dying.'[4] If this stunning statement is true then everything has changed and what Jesus said is of ultimate importance for all of us.

---

3. John 11:25, 26.
4. Hebrews 2:14, 15 [New Living Translation, 1996].

People loved listening to what Jesus had to say. His words were and still are the most profound that have ever been spoken. Those who heard him wondered if he might be the Messiah. They hoped he would deliver the Jewish nation from Roman oppression. When the religious leaders got wind of what people were saying, they sent the Temple guard to arrest him.[5] The guards found Jesus, but returned without him in custody. When asked why, much to the annoyance of their employers, they simply said, 'No one ever spoke the way this man does.'[6] Imagine if police officers were sent to Speakers' Corner in Hyde Park to arrest someone whom the authorities considered a rabble rouser. They don't arrest him, but instead leave him to carry on because they are so impressed by the way he speaks. Not a great career move!

Jesus' words were challenging and always provoked a response, which is why not everyone loved what he had to say. Even so, multitudes followed him wherever he went. These crowds were made up not just of the wealthy, the religious, the academics and the liberal elite but also the poor, the ne'er-do-wells, the uneducated and the marginalised. The latter loved listening to him because what he said gave them hope. Jesus himself said his words were spirit and life.[7] If his words in life were significant then how much more his words in death?

Malcolm Muggeridge, the journalist and author, once said that Jesus' death 'was manifestly the most famous death in history'.[8] Jesus was on the cross for some six hours and the

---

5. John 7:32.
6. John 7:46.
7. John 6:63.
8. Malcolm Muggeridge wrote in The Observer on 26 March 1967: 'One thing at least can be said with certainty about the crucifixion of Christ: It was manifestly the most famous death in history. No other death has aroused 100th part of the interest, or been remembered with 100th part of the intensity and concern...', quoted in Dick Tripp, *Why did Jesus die? What the Bible says about the Cross* (Wipf and Stock, 2014).

four Gospels record what happened and what he said. He didn't say much – not surprising in the light of what he was going through – but the seven things he did say are worth listening to. If Jesus was who he said he was (more of that later) and did what the Bible said he did, his last words must hold answers to the questions that both life and, more importantly, death pose. They do.

Jesus' seven cries from the cross have captivated me over many years. The more time I have spent contemplating what he said, the richer in meaning I have found his words. In this short book, my hope is to open your hearts and minds to what truly are famous last words!

CHAPTER 1

THE BIG PICTURE

'The Innocent Sufferer'

> *When they had crucified him, they divided up his clothes by casting lots. And sitting down, they kept watch over him there.*
>
> *(Matthew 27:35, 36)*

My 'do-it-yourself' skills have become the stuff of legend. However, God has kindly ensured that my unwarranted confidence in my own ability is counter-balanced by the certain disappointment of my wife, Annie. She is so sure of what is about to happen that she never stays at home when she hears those fateful words: 'I'm just going to sort out the . . .' She has learnt, through painful experience, that *just going to* and *sort out* should never come out of my mouth in close proximity to each other. She is rightly convinced that virtually all of the ensuing problems would have been resolved by three things. Using the right tools (instead of what she considers is a troubling reliance on 'old faithful', my trusty hammer), a modicum of common sense and, finally, reading the instructions before turning to 'old faithful'. Whilst Annie has concluded that the first two are probably beyond my limited capabilities, she still has what she feels is a reasonable expectation that I should read the instructions before I start one of my do-it-yourself ventures. She is of course right. Failure to grasp the big picture always leads to confusion and frustration.

For exactly the same reason, before we focus on what Jesus actually said on the cross, it is important that we understand the bigger picture. One of the important ground rules for understanding the Bible is that passages of scripture should be interpreted in light of other passages of scripture. This is why Jesus' last words need to be seen against the backdrop of the whole of the Bible, as well as the things Jesus specifically said and taught before he went to the cross. Only when we have done this can we fully appreciate the immensity of what he said while he was on the cross. In the four Gospels we have four eyewitness accounts of Jesus' last hours. The writers, Matthew, Mark, Luke and John, agree with one another on the main points of what happened that day. As you would expect with genuine eyewitness accounts of the same event, they don't all record the same details. These differences, however, are not material. Placing these four accounts against the broader canvas of the rest of scripture we start to see some common themes. These are going to give us a deeper appreciation of what Jesus was saying when he was on the cross. So what are some of these threads?

The unexpected silence

Matthew gives us lots of detail about what happened in the Garden of Gethsemane[9] and especially what happened when Jesus was arrested and stood before the High Priest, Caiaphas, and the Sanhedrin.[10] Remarkably, he even tells us about Peter's denial of Jesus.[11] When Matthew wrote his Gospel, 30 or so years after the events had happened, Peter was the leader of the quickly growing early Church. The fact that he recounts Peter's failure, and in such detail, is made even more astounding when we realise that all of the information on this shameful incident must have come from Peter himself. Matthew even goes to

---

9. Matthew 26:36-56. The Garden of Gethsemane is located on the Mount of Olives. This is where Jesus went to pray with his disciples the night before he was betrayed.
10. Matthew 26:57-68.
11. Matthew 26:69-75.

great lengths to tell us of Judas' remorse at his betrayal of Jesus, but also his ultimate lack of repentance and his grisly end.[12] He tells us what happened at Jesus' cross-examination by Pilate and the events that unfolded afterwards.[13] Matthew leaves no stone unturned as he reveals the determination of the religious leaders to have Jesus killed and exposes the fickle nature of the crowd. All of this is put on public display.

Yet when we come to the crucifixion itself, Matthew and the other Gospel writers are strangely silent. There is no detailed account of the gruesome nature of Jesus' death. Crucifixion was cruelly designed to cause intense and prolonged suffering. Whilst the Romans used it as a means of execution for criminals and rebels, the horror of crucifixion was a stark warning to all living under the 'Pax Romana'.[14] Roman peace was brutally enforced through fear. Cicero, the Roman writer, described crucifixion as a cruel and terrible punishment which was so degrading that most Roman citizens avoided talking about it.[15] Yet for the Roman soldiers it was just another day at the office, part of the routine of military duty. They had crucified hundreds of people.

The Gospel writers tell us that, prior to Jesus' crucifixion, he had been beaten and tortured.[16] Yet as the focus of events moves to Golgotha, the place of execution, all we are told is that they crucified him.[17] It seems that the writers considered that sufficient information for their readers. There is no detailed and bloody account of what the soldiers actually did. There is

---

12. Matthew 27:3-10.
13. Matthew 27:11-26.
14. The 'Pax Romana' referred to the 200 years or so of relative peace across the Roman Empire which started not long before the birth of Jesus.
15. Cited in John Stott, *The Cross of Christ* (InterVarsity Press, 1986), pp.24–5.
16. Luke 22:63.
17. Matthew 27:35.

almost uniform silence over the physical, mental, emotional and spiritual agonies that Jesus went through. Our fixation with the minutiae of what Jesus suffered, as demonstrated in Mel Gibson's film, *The Passion of the Christ*, is not supported by the Gospel writers.

At university, I remember the student Christian Union organising a week of events all about Jesus. The publicity simply said, 'And now for someone completely different.' One of the evening talks focused on the death of Jesus. Whilst I am sure that it was a reasonably accurate portrayal of the details of the crucifixion, it was certainly not for the faint-hearted. Even though they knew what actually happened, the Gospel writers said little because, as far as they were concerned, it was counter-productive. Marcus Loane, the twentieth-century theologian and author, suggests that Matthew and the other Gospel writers were comparatively silent on this issue because what happened that day affected them so deeply that they were only able to write about it with great restraint.[18] It is as if they couldn't bring themselves to tell us what they saw, or even dwell on the details. They knew they were standing on holy ground. Their silence reflected their sense of awe and reverence at what Jesus had done. It is clear that they didn't want the brutal details to, in any way, obscure what he accomplished for us on the cross.

The unusual script

We live in an increasingly litigious society built upon a blame culture. If truth be told, this is nothing new. Since time immemorial

---

18. Marcus Loane, *The Voice of the Cross* (Marshall, Morgan & Scott, 1956), p.17.

people have blame-shifted to avoid taking responsibility for their own actions. Yet not one of the Gospel writers seeks to attribute blame for what happened that day. Who was responsible? The Jews? Certainly there have been those through the centuries who have used this to encourage an anti-Semitic agenda. What about the Romans? Surely Pontius Pilate can't wash his hands of any involvement? And what about the religious leaders and the crowd? To one degree or another, they all had a part to play. However, the Bible makes it clear that, behind it all, God was at work.[19] Peter, preaching to the crowd that gathered on the Day of Pentecost in Jerusalem, put it like this: 'This man was handed over to you by God's set purpose and foreknowledge; and you, with the help of wicked men, put him to death by nailing him to the cross.'[20]

To be honest, I am just grateful it was nothing to do with me! Unfortunately, it becomes clear from scripture that actually I am involved. Jesus' death had something to do with all of us. Probably the most well-known of all Bible verses[21] reminds us that God so loved the world – and all of us are part of the world – that he sent his Son, Jesus, to sort out the problem we had created. The Bible calls our rebellion, our determined independence from the God who created us, 'sin'. It is only as we grasp what this really means that we start to see how precarious our situation really is. If the Bible is true then God is Almighty. He knows everything. He created us and the universe in which we live. He deserves our worship. In fact, he has every right to expect our worship! To turn our back on the One who created us and who still sustains us is treachery.

---

19. Isaiah 53:10.
20. Acts 2:23.
21. John 3:16.

This is not a word we like to hear. All of us have offended God.[22] There is only one way to deal with rebels. It is not the happy-ever-after ending that we hope for and think we deserve. Far from it.

Yet, in an extraordinary turn of events, the Bible says God has held back from judgement and gone to great lengths to draw us back into relationship with himself. However, whilst God is love,[23] he is also just.[24] He cannot be one without the other, which is why our sin could not be overlooked. God's love and justice are satisfied at the cross. God's love caused him to send his Son to pay the price for our rebellion. This is the reason why all of us had a part to play in Jesus' death. Mel Gibson directed, but didn't star in the film, *The Passion of the Christ*. Unbeknownst to many, though, he did have a small cameo role. In the scene in which Jesus is being crucified, all we see is a Roman soldier's hands nailing Jesus to the cross. Those hands belonged to Mel Gibson. By this small act he wanted to convey that he was part of the reason why Jesus had to die. Our sin put him on the cross.

The innocent sufferer

Jesus was no martyr to a cause. He was not the leader of the bleeding heart brigade. Rather, he was an innocent yet willing victim. Matthew emphasises the illegalities of the trial of Jesus. If we needed any convincing, Jesus' trial before the Jewish Sanhedrin was held at night and during a festival. The death sentence was reached within a day without there being any

---
22. Romans 3:23.
23. 1 John 4:16.
24. Romans 3:26.

counsel for the defence. The 'conviction' – if we dare call it that – was based on the flimsiest of evidence from unreliable witnesses.[25] It was a travesty of justice.

Bizarrely, several of the people involved in Jesus' death sentence were convinced that Jesus was innocent of the charges being brought against him. This motley crew included Judas,[26] who had betrayed him for personal gain, and Pilate[27] himself (as well as his wife)![28] Yet none of them could change what was about to happen because, as we've seen, behind the scenes, God was at work. God had planned that Jesus would die on a cross, even before humankind turned its back on him in the Garden of Eden.[29]

If God does hold us accountable for our own thoughts and actions, then we are all in serious trouble. What hope do we have? We need someone to represent us before God.[30] God is perfect or, as the Bible says, God is *holy*, so who can stand in God's presence and speak up for us? The psalmist asks a similar question: 'Who may ascend the hill of the Lord and stand in his holy presence? Only he who has clean hands and a pure heart.'[31] Our sin requires the intervention of someone who is innocent before God. Throughout the Old Testament, the writers look forward to the arrival of a willing, innocent 'servant' who would stand in the gap between God and us.[32] Jesus came to be that servant.[33] He knew from the beginning that he was going to die. His death was no accident. Isaiah prophesying about Jesus'

---

25. Matthew 26:59, 60.
26. Matthew 27:4.
27. Luke 23:13-16.
28. Matthew 27:19.
29. Revelation 13:8.
30. Job 9:33.
31. Psalm 24:3, 4.
32. Isaiah 59:16.
33. Philippians 2:7, 8.

death hundreds of years before it happened said: 'Yet it was the Lord's will to crush him and cause him to suffer . . .'[34] Jesus was an innocent sufferer.

The perfect substitute

Despite my love of football, I would never want to manage a team. I'd rather remain an armchair expert. It seems to me that managing is a thankless task. One of the many challenges is being able to introduce the right substitute to change the game before it is too late. Every manager wants to bring on the perfect substitute who has an immediate impact. Most of the time, as far as football is concerned, it involves more luck than judgement.

Matthew's account is full of irony. It was 'normal practice' at the Passover Feast for the governor to release a prisoner. Pilate sought to use this fact to engineer Jesus' release. However, the pressure put on him by the baying crowd caused him to buckle and release Barabbas, a notorious criminal, instead of Jesus. Barabbas' name meant 'son of the father'. The irony was that there was another 'Son of the Father' on centre stage that day. Yet of the two, the criminal was set free whilst the innocent Son of God died in his place. Humanly speaking, it was not a great substitution!

Every prisoner had a charge sheet which explained why they were being executed. It was hung round their neck and then nailed to the cross as a deterrent to others. Pilate, possibly getting his own back on the religious leaders, ensured the charge sheet simply said: 'This is Jesus, the King of the Jews.'[35]

---

34. Isaiah 53:10.
35. Matthew 27:37.

He had no idea how right he was! By recording this detail, Matthew was reminding everyone that the people of Jerusalem killed their own king. Yet Jesus' death highlighted a far more significant substitution that was going on that day. From what we have already seen, I don't think you will be surprised.

Jesus died in place of each and every one of us. All of us, like Barabbas, stand guilty before a holy God. Like Barabbas, we are all sons of our father. Spiritually our father is Adam. Each of us has inherited our father Adam's rebellion against God in our spiritual DNA. All of us would remain eternally separated from God without God's own intervention. The only way out starts with us acknowledging our sin. The Dutch painter Rembrandt, in his work *The Three Crosses*, which is his representation of the death of Christ, apparently painted himself into the crowd in the shadows around the cross. In doing so he was conveying that Jesus' death involved him. Jesus, the 'Son of the Father', came as a substitute for each one of us. He took our place and our punishment. Martyn Lloyd-Jones, an influential evangelical minister of the twentieth century, summed it up when he said: 'At Calvary, God was laying your iniquity [wickedness] on his Son. God was taking your sins and punishing them in him. His blood was shed that your sins might be blotted out. That is the only answer and the only explanation for Christ's death.'[36]

As we reflect on this scene, it is hard not to be overwhelmed. The Son of God – who had never done any wrong, who had only ever loved the unlovely and who had come to show us that God loved us – died as a criminal in our place. Over the centuries many people have had their lives changed as they have contemplated what Jesus did for them.

---

36. Martyn Lloyd-Jones, *Authentic Christianity* (Banner of Truth, 1999), p.267.

German-born Count Nicholas von Zinzendorf was one such person. Von Zinzendorf, a wealthy young nobleman, already believed in Jesus. He was stopping over in Düsseldorf on his way to Paris when, having some time on his hands, he decided to visit the city's art gallery. While there he saw for the first time Sternberg's picture of the crucified Christ known as *Ecce Homo* ('Behold the man'). Underneath the picture, in Latin, was written: 'I did this for you, what will you do for me?' Von Zinzendorf was transfixed. He sat there for hours overwhelmed by Christ's death on his behalf. In those moments the destiny of his life was changed. From that day forward everything he was, and everything he had, he gave in the service of Christ. Afterwards he simply said, 'I have one passion; it is Jesus, Jesus only.' Subsequently, he was involved in founding a movement of followers of Jesus known as the Moravians, whose passion for Christ still shines brightly through the pages of history.[37]

The acceptable sacrifice

More than any other Gospel writer, Matthew draws our attention to the blood of Christ. We read about it in relation to Judas, the chief priests and Pilate as well as the crowd in Jerusalem on the day that Jesus was crucified.[38] His intention was to show that the shedding of Jesus' blood replaced, once and for all, the shedding of the blood of the Passover lamb which had long been part of the way the Jewish nation related to God. Throughout the time of the Old Testament, God accepted a substitute for the sins of his people. Instead

---

37. Loane, *The Voice of the Cross*, p.19.
38. Matthew 27.

of punishing them, he accepted the sacrifice of a spotless and blemish-free lamb. Before we switch off because this seems barbaric and a relic of a bygone age, remember that all of this was pointing towards the day when God would provide an altogether better sacrifice.

God's amazing plan to save us was that his Son would be the once-for-all acceptable sacrifice for our sins. After Jesus' death, no more sacrifice was needed.[39] No wonder John the Baptist called Jesus the 'Lamb of God, who takes away the sin of the world!'[40] The events at the cross were the beginning of a new way for us to relate to God. Jesus' blood was to be 'poured out for many for the forgiveness of sins'.[41] This way is now open to all of us. No one is beyond God's grace. All we need to do is put our faith and trust in what Christ has done and we can draw near to the living God. Paul reminds us in Ephesians: 'But now in Christ Jesus you who once were far away have been brought near through the blood of Christ.'[42] This is the culmination of the gospel ('good news') because without the shedding of blood there can be no forgiveness of sin.[43]

Threads of the tapestry

If we view each aspect of the gospel separately, they may appear unrelated, rather like random coloured threads that we find at the back of a tapestry. Viewing each thread and their relationship to one another can be a complicated process and difficult to follow. It is only when we turn the tapestry over

---

39. Hebrews 9:11-14, 26.
40. John 1:29.
41. Matthew 26:28.
42. Ephesians 2:13.
43. Hebrews 9:22.

that we appreciate the skill of the master weaver. Suddenly we see the big picture in vibrant colour. Until we view it from the perspective of the master weaver it all can be very confusing. Contemplating God's big picture we see the good news in all its fullness. The 66 books of the Bible, written by a multitude of different people over thousands of years, weave one story from beginning to end:

God created us, loved us and enjoyed relationship with us. We spoiled everything by believing the great lie that we didn't need God. It wasn't true. We were made to worship God. Amazingly, instead of writing us off, God, being always loving, committed to bringing us home. Yet, being always just, he couldn't turn a blind eye to our sin. He showed us the way to live, a standard that was impossible for us to keep. In doing so, he was revealing our need of grace. At just the right time God put his rescue plan into action. He sent his Son, Jesus, to become a man. The perfect man. God wouldn't compromise his holiness or his love. Sin had to be dealt a death blow. Jesus would do it once for all. As he hung on the cross between God and man, he paid the terrible price of our sin. His arms reached out to all who would receive him. His cries from the cross tell the whole story – well, nearly the whole story.

Proof of victory

There's nothing worse than watching a supposedly 'must-win contest' and then finding at the end that the result is inconclusive. Both sides claim they won. In reality no one is sure. It is particularly important to establish who won if the contest is a matter of life and death! Jesus' cries on the cross may well be profound yet they are meaningless if he didn't in fact rise from the dead. The proof that what he said is true is in the fact of his resurrection. Paul says that if Jesus hasn't been raised from the dead then our faith is futile and we are still in our sins.[44]

Having sat with many people following the death of a loved one, I have heard people say all sorts of things in the emotion of the moment. One in particular stands out. The person concerned was saying to their recently departed loved one that they were 'going to keep on fighting death'. Whilst I am not really sure what they meant, the truth is that we don't need to fight death if Jesus has already defeated it through his death and resurrection. This is the good news of the gospel.[45]

I wonder whether we cling to this life so desperately because we are not absolutely sure of Jesus' victory and what it means. Paul was absolutely convinced. He said, 'For to me, to live is Christ and to die is gain.'[46] It is a deeply challenging statement. Could I say the same? It is essential that we are totally persuaded that Jesus rose from the dead, because it changes everything. As we consider Jesus' cries from the cross, we must do so in the light of what Jesus himself says: 'Do not be afraid. I am the First and the Last. I am the Living One; I was dead, and behold I am alive for ever and ever! And I hold the keys of death and Hades.'[47]

---

44. 1 Corinthians 15:17.
45. In the Bible the phrase 'the Gospels' refers to the first four books of the New Testament, namely Matthew, Mark, Luke and John. All of them are accounts of the events surrounding Jesus' birth, life, death and resurrection. The word 'gospel' actually means 'good news'. Hence the gospel is the good news about Jesus.
46. Philippians 1:21.
47. Revelation 1:17, 18.

CHAPTER 2

JUST FORGIVENESS

'What Abraham Saw'

> *Two other men, both criminals, were also led out with him to be executed. When they came to the place called the Skull, there they crucified him, along with the criminals – one on his right, the other on his left. Jesus said, 'Father, forgive them, for they do not know what they are doing.' And they divided up his clothes by casting lots.*
>
> *(Luke 23:32-34)*

Last words can be powerful. They have the potential to be both poignant and devastating. 'I love you' from a dying partner or parent can go some way to make up for mistakes made over many years. The opposite can also be true. At the end people can dwell on a life well spent or on the regrets of what was or what might have been. Unsurprisingly, I am not aware of any recorded last words of people wishing they'd worked harder or spent more time in the office. Certainly not any office that I ever worked in!

Having said this, I would expect the final words of those who are about to be executed to carry a different tone. From the little I have read they do. Some people are angry. A few are indignant, still pleading their innocence to the last. Others are clearly trying to be brave which sometimes results in inappropriate humour. I'm sure all are terrified, whether they admit it or not. My only surprise is that more are not sorry for their actions.

Then there is Jesus

No one ever said anything remotely like what Jesus said. As he died on the cross he wasn't angry, indignant or fearful. He wasn't repentant because he had nothing to be sorry for. He offered no word in his own defence and made no attempt to proclaim his innocence. He blamed no one. Instead, remarkably, he asked God to forgive all those who were responsible for him being crucified! I have sat with numbers of people who have said unexpectedly kind things before they died, but nothing compares to the significance of what Jesus said.

Some time ago I had the privilege of spending a few hours with a friend in their fifties who was dying from cancer. His concern was not for himself but for those he loved. I was left with a detailed list of what he wanted me to say at the funeral service to people who meant a lot to him. As he struggled to breathe he was determined to tell me his life story, including about his very sad and difficult childhood. His father, who should have protected him as he was growing up, had allowed him to be mistreated. Over the ensuing 40 years he had managed to overcome the trauma and had lived a very full life. He had moved on in every area except one. He couldn't forgive his father for the way he had abandoned him. One of his last wishes was that his father should not come to his funeral. Being human, after hearing the story and sensing his heartache, I could understand why. Yet the pain of what had happened was like a prison cell – not for his father, but for him. I have no idea whether his father was even aware of what he had allowed to happen to his son all those years before.

Unforgiveness can keep the damaged person behind self-imposed bars.

We can all understand how the last words of those who've been unfairly treated can be tainted with resentment and even anger. But forgiveness? This is what marks Jesus' words as extraordinary. Forgiveness is a costly and precious gift. We are about to find out just how costly and just how precious. As we explore what Luke has recorded, we will find it is more significant than we could ever have imagined.

An act of significance

Jesus, having been sentenced to death by crucifixion, was taken with two other convicted criminals to be executed. We know nothing about these two men save that, by the admission of one of them, they were guilty as charged.[48] As we have already seen, Jesus was not. His sentence of death was passed by a judge who, having declared him innocent, caved in under the pressure of a baying mob.[49] Yet the significance of what was about to happen had nothing to do with a miscarriage of justice. If that were the case it would have been just another in a long line of such incidents throughout the pages of history. No, the significance lay in the fact that the details of Jesus' death were in the public domain long before it took place.

Around 700 years before the events of this day, a Jewish prophet called Isaiah foretold it all in remarkable detail. He described how one day God's chosen Servant would appear on the scene. However, instead of receiving adulation from the people that God had sent him to help, he would be despised and rejected. The key passage in Isaiah tells us that there would be nothing in his appearance or bearing that would draw people to him. Whilst he would be ordinary to look at, he would die doing something astonishing. Isaiah prophesied that he would die in the place of all those who had offended God. Wrongly,

---

48. Luke 23:41.
49. Luke 23:20-25.

the people would think God was punishing him whereas, in fact, he would die in the place of everyone else, including Isaiah, and us.

What was Isaiah's explanation? The nub of what he says is that we have all lived without honouring the God who created us, or as he puts it, we have 'turned to our own way'. This Servant would be led silently to a criminal's execution just like a sacrificial lamb, which was exactly the point. Finally, even though it would look like the people had executed an innocent man, Isaiah said it was God who had planned for this to happen. Through this Servant's death, many would be made right with God.[50]

The ignominy of Jesus' death in between two villains is the part-fulfilment of Isaiah's prophecy that the Messiah would be 'numbered with the transgressors'.[51] Whatever you think about prophecy, the similarities between what Isaiah says and how Jesus died are remarkable. The cynic in us all looks for signs of a conspiracy. Yet over the centuries that have come and gone there is no substantive evidence that warrants us not taking this at face value. No one could control the events surrounding their own execution so as to ensure they fulfilled what someone said 700 years earlier. Either it is a coincidence of epic proportions or God is at work. We may not understand it but it is difficult not to conclude that in front of us is an act of great significance.

A place of significance

Some places are memorable for all the wrong reasons. Football for a schoolboy in Swansea meant that, at some point, you

---

50. Isaiah 53:1-12.
51. Isaiah 53:12.

would have to play away at Paradise Park. The name conjures up all sorts of idyllic images. However, in reality, nowhere could have been further from paradise. A muddy field on top of windswept Townhill, with a guaranteed 'warm welcome' from the home side!

Several years ago I had the privilege of visiting Israel and spending a day in Jerusalem. I stood on the Temple Mount, sat on the Mount of Olives and walked along part of the Via Dolorosa (the route on which Jesus was apparently taken to the cross). The Old City is surprisingly small and compact by modern-day standards but everywhere you go it oozes history. It felt like the pages of the Bible were coming alive in front of me. Anywhere that appeared to be of any religious significance now seemed to be the site of a church. Yet as I walked outside the walls of the Old City I came close to the place, many believe, where Jesus was crucified. Part of it is now being used as a bus depot. There is nothing that indicates that this had been a place of any significance.

Luke tells us that Jesus was taken to the place known locally as 'Golgotha' which meant 'the place of the skull' ('Calvary' in Latin). More than likely it had been given its name because it was the place of execution for common criminals. No doubt it had seen many executions. It was located on the hillside outside the city walls on a public thoroughfare. Golgotha was the place chosen by the Roman authorities for Jesus' execution, authorised by Pontius Pilate. Despite all of this, behind the actions of men, God was working out his great plan of salvation. The Bible tells us that this rocky hilltop was the place of sacrifice ordained by God from the foundation of the world.[52]

---

52. John 19:17, 18; Revelation 13:8.

Why is the place of Jesus' crucifixion significant? As we read through the Old Testament, we come across men and women whom God involved in his purposes as he was fulfilling his great plan. Among all of these people, Abraham stands out. God called him to leave his homeland, a place called Ur of the Chaldeans, located in modern-day Iraq. At face value, Abraham did not appear a great candidate. He came from a family of moon worshippers.[53] However, when God spoke to him he obeyed unquestioningly. Beyond anything else, obedience was what God was looking for. Abraham left his wider family and community behind in Ur without having any idea where he was going. Over the coming months and years, he trusted God to lead him. Nevertheless, there existed an overwhelming sadness for Abraham and his wife, Sarah. The one thing that they longed for was an heir. Sarah was barren. To their delight, God promised them they would have a son and that through him Abraham would have descendants as numerous as the stars in the night sky.[54] Abraham believed that what God had said would happen.

Yet the years passed by and nothing changed. When humanly it was too late, God brought about what he had promised them all those years before. Sarah conceived and gave birth to Isaac. He was the child that God had promised them. All was well with the world . . . or so they thought. Then one day God spoke to Abraham. He told him to take Isaac to a place he would show him and there he was to sacrifice his son!

Many people have struggled with this passage in Genesis. If God is a God of love, how can he ask Abraham to do this?

---

53. Joshua 24:2.
54. Genesis 15:4-6.

What made Abraham even contemplate doing it? I have no easy answers but what does stand out is Abraham's faith in God.[55] Irrespective of what he was feeling, he obeyed. He took his one and only son, Isaac, to the region of Moriah. We are told that he saw in the distance the place of sacrifice.[56] If you don't know the story, just as Abraham was about to sacrifice his son God stops him.[57] We are told that God was testing him. He provided a ram for the sacrifice instead of Isaac.

Hundreds of years later, Mount Moriah would be where the city of Jerusalem was established.[58] It would be here that King Solomon would build a temple for the worship of God. I have long wondered whether the place where Abraham intended to offer his son as a sacrifice was where God would, in the fullness of time, sacrifice his own beloved Son. The writer of the book of Genesis tells us that in response to this incident it was said, 'On the mountain of the Lord it will be provided.'[59] This place was clearly recognised to be of enormous significance. I wonder if Abraham had some inkling that God was saying, 'you don't need to offer your only son because a day will come when on this mountain I will sacrifice my one and only Son'. If so, God was giving Abraham an insight into his great plan of salvation which would, one day, unfold on the cross.

Much later John, in his Gospel, tells us that Jesus said, 'Abraham rejoiced at the thought of seeing my day; he saw it and was glad.'[60] Abraham is referred to as a prophet but how did he see Jesus' day?[61] What did Jesus mean? Personally, I believe

---

55. Hebrews 11:17-19.
56. Genesis 22:4.
57. Genesis 22:12.
58. 2 Chronicles 3:1.
59. Genesis 22:14.
60. John 8:56.
61. 1 Peter 1:10-12.

that Jesus was referring to the incident we have just read about. The place to which God led Abraham was distinctive because we are told that he saw it from a distance. Moreover, I am sure that Abraham came to understand something of God's great redemptive love because God provided a substitute for his son Isaac. We can only speculate about what Abraham 'saw' but, whatever he 'saw', we are told it made him glad!

Words of significance

The first words that Jesus uttered on the cross (and as we will subsequently see, the last) are a prayer. They remind us of his unwavering trust in God as he reached the climax of what he had come to earth to do. He knew that this would end in his physical death. He was also fully aware of the awful nature of what he would experience. If there was any other way that God's plan could have been accomplished, God the Father and Jesus would have taken it.[62] Yet in the midst of all the physical pain and emotional anguish, Jesus prayed not for himself but for those who were responsible for putting him on the cross. Each phrase is rich with meaning.

'Father'

I didn't appreciate what it meant to have a father until I no longer had one. I always knew that my father loved me, even if he rarely told me so. Our relationship through my teenage years was fraught with difficulties, mostly generated by me. After I

---

62. Matthew 26:39.

left home, our relationship improved, only for it to end abruptly as a result of a road traffic accident. I had no idea of how to handle the situation or the emotions that it provoked. I felt too young not to have a father. Six weeks later, on the spur of the moment, my brother-in-law and I went to a meeting organised by a local church in Southampton. The publicity simply said that an American couple with a recognised prophetic gift were speaking. If I'm being honest, I went with a measure of cynicism. It disappeared when I was singled out of a crowd of about 200 people and told that God had something to say to me: 'God says he is going to be a Father to you.' The phrase was then repeated around five times. Anyone else in the room that night could have been forgiven for thinking it was hardly an earth-shattering revelation. Little could anyone know of the impact those few words would have on my life. I may no longer have had an earthly father but God was promising that he would be a Father to me. Twenty-eight years have come and gone. Throughout all that time I have known the deep comfort of the fathering of Almighty God.

People's life experiences colour their understanding of fatherhood. Many people struggle to relate to the concept of God being their Father because of the way their earthly father treated them. For them the word 'father' stirs up, amongst other things, feelings of rejection, anger and low self-esteem. Lives have been ruined as a result. Sadly, we live in a world full of flawed fathers. My father was flawed. And much to my disappointment, so am I. God, however, is the perfect Father.[63] Jesus' first word on the cross is an antidote to the ache in the human heart to know the true Father's love. Only at the cross can this ache be healed.

---

63. Matthew 5:48.

The word for Father that Jesus used was 'Abba'. Today we would use the word 'Dad'. It conveyed a close and intimate relationship and demonstrated Jesus' love and trust of God. When he prayed, and he prayed a lot, Jesus always called God 'Father'. In turn, God called Jesus 'his beloved Son'.[64] For all eternity, God has been the Father and Jesus has always been the Son.

In his agony on the cross Jesus speaks to his Father. Under pressure we find out what people really believe. Jesus himself had said that out of the overflow of the heart the mouth speaks.[65] If we squeeze a sponge, what comes out is only what the sponge has absorbed. When Jesus was under pressure and his life was literally being squeezed out of his physical body, what came out of his mouth was what was in his heart. In the darkest and bleakest moment of his short life, Jesus prayed to his Father. One of the wonders of the cross is that Jesus' death and subsequent resurrection have opened up the possibility for us to have the same intimate relationship with God. However difficult life is for us and whatever trials we are facing, in the midst of it all through Jesus we can know the deep comfort of God as our Father. This would be a good moment to reflect on whether we know for certain that God is our Father and that he is good.

'Forgive them'

Forgiving the young man who had driven the car that caused my father's death was helped by the knowledge that in the moment

---

64. Matthew 3:17.
65. Matthew 12:34.

he had made a terrible error of judgement. I knew I had made mistakes while driving which, by the grace of God, had not had such devastating consequences. However, it is not always that easy. Whenever I hear of someone who has been systematically and deliberately abused publicly forgiving the person who has hurt them I wonder whether I could do the same in comparable circumstances. Throughout history there are examples of men and women who have forgiven those who have committed some of the most heinous crimes against humanity. They are remarkable people. So why do Jesus' words eclipse them all?

Jesus, whilst completely human, is not our peer. He is the eternal Son of God. He created all things and sustains the whole cosmos.[66] Jesus never did anything wrong.[67] He lived his life only doing good[68] and always for the benefit of others. Yet he unjustly suffered a cruel and barbaric death at the hands of those he had created. However, at no point did he cry out to his Father for justice or vengeance. Rather, he asked that God would forgive them. In doing so, he fulfilled another part of Isaiah's prophecy that we looked at earlier.[69]

We struggle to conceive how anyone in such circumstances could genuinely mean this. The Christian author Philip Greenslade sums this feeling up when he says: 'The reason we are baffled and astonished when some people find it in their hearts to forgive those who have grievously wronged them, and the reason why we sympathise with even good and godly people when they cannot find it in their hearts to forgive – is precisely because forgiving one's enemies seems difficult, even

---

66. John 1:1-3, 14.
67. Hebrews 4:15.
68. Acts 10:38.
69. Isaiah 53:12.

impossible, to contemplate. And that's because it is!'[70] Here at the cross we see amazing grace, the Son of God praying for the forgiveness of those who were instrumental in his execution! Jesus was practising what he preached.[71]

Yet there is something else which is surprising. As we read through the accounts of Jesus' life in the four Gospels we come across numerous occasions when Jesus forgave people's sins.[72] The religious people of the day, the teachers of the law, were outraged when he told people that their sins were forgiven. They accused him of blasphemy. Only God could forgive sin. So here's the rub – if Jesus knew that he was God and had the right to forgive sin, why does he ask his Father to forgive them? Why doesn't he do it himself?

The explanation is simple. It was God the Father's plan[73] to put to death his Son as our substitute. As we have already seen, it was the only way for humankind's rebellion to be forgiven. Martyn Lloyd-Jones explains that a just and holy God cannot simply say, 'I forgive you' and sweep the matter under the carpet. If God could have forgiven us that easily he would have done so.[74] Each one of us will one day stand before God and have to give an account for the life he gave us. All of us have fallen short of God's standards, which is why we need forgiveness. In terms of living the way God intends for us to live, we all miss the mark. We are incapable of dealing with our sin ourselves which is why Jesus had to pay the price so that we might be forgiven.[75] He didn't plead with his Father to forgive. He knew his Father would forgive.

---

70. Philip Greenslade, *Voice from the Hills* (CWR, 2008), p.128.
71. Matthew 5:43-45.
72. Matthew 9:2; Mark 2:5-12; Luke 7:48.
73. Isaiah 53:10; Acts 2:23.
74. Martyn Lloyd-Jones, *Saved in Eternity* (Crossway Books, 1988), p.99.
75. 2 Corinthians 5:21.

It is pride that convinces us that we are not all that bad and that God will accept us just as we are. Pride always causes us to miss out on the grace that could be ours. It is our sin that caused the Son of God to go to the cross and pray, 'Father, forgive them.' Do we know that we have been forgiven? God doesn't automatically forgive each and every one of us. Forgiveness, once sought, has to be given freely but also has to be received. It is a gift that is available only through what Jesus has done on the cross. There are telltale signs that we have received forgiveness. Jesus said that those who realise how much they've been forgiven love much.[76] Forgiven people love God with all they have.[77] This is challenging. Maybe when we hold back on loving God it is because deep down we don't appreciate the extent of our sin and the cost of our forgiveness.

Once we understand this, we are provoked to love others in the same way that God has loved us. We freely forgive others as we have been forgiven. Forgiveness, however hard – and sometimes it is incredibly hard – is a sign that we have received the grace of God. It is never a one-off decision. We have to keep making the same decision to forgive moment by moment, hour by hour and day by day. The only way we will be able to let go of unforgiveness in our hearts is by living in the grace of God.

Unforgiveness is like a monkey trap. The trap has a hole just big enough for the monkey's paw. The monkey cannot remove its paw without letting go of the piece of fruit, which is there as the bait. It is caught by its own greed. Likewise when we hold on to unforgiveness it stops us from being able to experience the freedom that forgiveness brings.[78]

---

76. Luke 7:47.
77. Matthew 22:37.
78. Matthew 18:21-35.

'For they know not what they do'

Really? It seems to me that everyone knew very well what they were doing! Judas betrayed him. The religious leaders plotted and schemed to kill him. Pilate washed his hands of him. Herod had him beaten. The Roman soldiers nailed him to the cross. The crowd cried out for his death. They were all aware of what they were doing. We too are all implicated in his death. If we had been in Jerusalem that first Good Friday, I think we probably would have been in the crowd crying, 'Crucify him!' If we think otherwise we are deceiving ourselves.

So what did Jesus think they didn't know? Very simply, if they'd known that Jesus was God's Son, Paul tells us, they 'would not have crucified the Lord of glory'.[79] Don't be fooled, though, into thinking ignorance is a line of defence.[80] The crowds in Jerusalem found it was no excuse.[81] Albert Speer, one of Hitler's aides, when asked about the death camps allegedly said, 'I didn't know but I could have found out.' The Bible is clear that a person who offends God can only receive forgiveness when they recognise that what they have done is wrong. This is the start of repentance which involves turning to Jesus and endeavouring to live in a way that pleases him. Anyone who refuses to turn to Christ will face the consequences of their own actions.

The American pastor and author John Piper suggests that Jesus was saying they were guilty for not understanding what they were doing.[82] They thought they were innocent. In fact

---

79. 1 Corinthians 2:8.
80. Acts 3:13-15.
81. Numbers 15:22-29.
82. 'Father, forgive, for we know what we are doing', 27 January 2002, by John Piper. ©Desiring God Foundation. Source: desiringGod.org

THROUGH

'Just Forgiveness'

they were guilty because they failed to realise the significant part they played in Jesus being put to death.

Let's not make the same mistake and think we are not guilty before a holy God. Instead, let's remember the One who hung where we deserve to hang and has asked his Father to forgive us! What amazing grace!

Lasting significance

Let's finish by summing up the lasting significance of what Jesus said. The Apostle John explains our need for forgiveness, 'If we claim to be without sin, we deceive ourselves and the truth is not in us. If we confess our sins, he is faithful and just and will forgive us our sins and purify us from all unrighteousness. If we claim we have not sinned, we make him out to be a liar and his word is not in us.'[83] God can never forgive us just because he is loving (which he is) but he will forgive us because he is just. Jesus has paid the penalty for our sin. If we put our faith in Jesus, God must forgive us. If he forgives us, he will accept us into his presence when we close our eyes on this life. Now that is good news.

C. H. Spurgeon, the nineteenth-century English preacher, put it in his own inimitable style:

> *Yet, nevertheless, it is a truth that, because God is just, he must forgive every sinner who confesses his sin. And if he did not – and mark, it is a bold thing to say, but it is warranted by the text – if a sinner should be led truly and solemnly*

---

83. 1 John 1:8-10.

> *to make confession of his sins and cast himself on Christ, if God did not forgive him, then he were not the God that he is represented to be in the Word of God: he would be unjust, and . . . God forbid, such a thing must not, cannot be.[84]*

Just forgiveness indeed.

---

84. Charles Spurgeon preaching on Sunday morning, 29 May 1859, slightly paraphrased by the author.

CHAPTER 3

FIRST MAN HOME[85]

'The Bronze Serpent'

---

85. Philip Greenslade in *Voice from the Hills* uses the phrase 'first one home'.

> *One of the criminals who hung there hurled insults at him: 'Aren't you the Christ? Save yourself and us!' But the other criminal rebuked him. 'Don't you fear God,' he said, 'since you are under the same sentence? We are punished justly, for we are getting what our deeds deserve. But this man has done nothing wrong.' Then he said, 'Jesus, remember me when you come into your kingdom.' Jesus answered him, 'I tell you the truth, today you will be with me in paradise.'*
>
> (Luke 23:39-43)

I have great memories from growing up in Swansea. There were about ten boys living within a couple of hundred yards of one another, who used to play in the street outside my house. Whilst we loved it, I'm not sure that the neighbours were quite as positive. In truth I'm glad they, and especially my parents, never found out what some of the 'games' involved. For the most part though, we had a simple schedule. Winter was football. Summer was cricket. In the evenings we played Mob. Mob was best played in the twilight. It essentially required reaching 'the mobbing post' (aka the lamp post outside the front of my house) without being caught by the person whose turn it was to be 'on'. There were no other rules. Nothing was sacrosanct. Deceit, skulduggery, neighbours' back gardens and garage roofs were all fair game in the race to be the first man home.

Life is not a game. Heroic attempts to get home, even when they fail, are the stuff of legend. They are the focus of many well-known films, songs, works of literature and pieces of art. Many people have found themselves lost and far from home, wishing they could turn the clock back. Two of the three men being crucified outside Jerusalem that Friday morning had reached the point of no return. They would have done anything to be able to go home but they'd been caught, tried and found guilty. Luke calls them wrongdoers but the other Gospel writers are blunter. They describe them as robbers or bandits.[86] More likely they were zealots, revolutionaries whose crimes funded insurrection against the Romans. Now they were paying the ultimate price for their actions. Jesus was different. He had made no attempt to avoid the horror of being crucified. In fact, he viewed it as his Father's plan. Jesus knew he was going home.

This is the only time on the cross where we find Jesus involved in dialogue. He has a short but profound conversation with one of these two thieves. This was one of the things that the religious leaders found so offensive about Jesus. Whilst he had little time for those who kept all the religious rules and rituals, he willingly associated with those that they considered to be the dregs of Jewish society. This was why they regularly accused him of being a 'friend of sinners'.[87] It was one of the worst insults that could be thrown at someone who was supposed to be godly. To their irritation, Jesus seemed to love the 'slur' and made no attempt to stop mixing with tax collectors, prostitutes, lepers and the like. He always made time for those who came to him when their lives were in an utter mess. At the last, here on the cross, we find that there is still hope for the hopeless. No one is beyond the grace of God. Yet, as we are about to see, this one man's encounter with Jesus didn't have a promising start.

---

86. Greek 'lestai' which was also used of Barabbas in John 18:40.
87. Matthew 11:19.

The ridicule

It was the American novelist Mark Twain who said, 'No god and no religion can survive ridicule.'[88] If he was right then the cross should have been the beginning and the end of Christianity. Everyone, apart from a few of Jesus' heartbroken followers who watched on in silence, showered him with ridicule and contempt. Those that passed by taunted him.[89] The religious leaders mocked him,[90] smugly believing they had finally got their man. Bizarrely, both thieves joined in. Mark tells us that they 'heaped insults on him'.[91] Clearly there is no honour amongst thieves – albeit Jesus was no thief.

It seems evident from what Luke says that one of the two criminals continued to rail at Jesus. He knew that people had been saying that Jesus might be the Messiah. As we've seen, the written charge,[92] nailed on Jesus' cross at Pilate's request, simply said: 'This is the King of the Jews.'[93] Tragically, this criminal's last words were full of mocking scorn: 'if you are the Christ, save yourself and us'. As far as most people looking on were concerned, the punishment being meted out to Jesus proved that he was no Messiah.

Even if these people believed Jesus was deluded, didn't he at least deserve a modicum of pity? As we contemplate what unfolded that day, we get an insight into the ugly side of human nature. A brief skim through the pages of history reveals that this was no 'one-off' incident but is, in fact, a flaw running through the whole of humankind. Years ago I read Charles

---

88. Mark Twain's *Notebook*, 1935.
89. Matthew 27:39, 40; Mark 15:29, 30.
90. Matthew 27:41-43; Mark 15:31, 32.
91. Mark 15:32.
92. Greek 'titulus'.
93. Luke 23:38.

Dickens' *A Tale of Two Cities*. Dickens' description of the inhumanity of the crowds that gathered to watch the gruesome spectacle of 'Madame la Guillotine' was haunting. It seems that nothing has changed over the centuries. We fool ourselves if we think that we are better than those who have gone before us. All of us are capable of doing the worst of things.

Jesus is still the focus of ridicule today. To the majority, most of whom know nothing about him, Jesus' name is a swear word. I wouldn't have to walk far through my home city of Winchester to hear his name being used in this way. How ironic that what is used as a curse has such a deep and rich meaning. His parents were told to call him 'Jesus' before he was born, 'because he will save his people from their sins'.[94] The name is the Greek form of Joshua, which means 'the Lord saves'. Our ridicule of Jesus displays the depth of humanity's rebellion against its Creator. We desperately need saving and Jesus is the only one who can do it. The Bible makes it clear that those who put their trust in him have been saved,[95] are being saved[96] and one day will finally be saved.[97]

D. A. Carson, the Canadian theologian and author, refers to another irony in his book *Scandalous*, when he talks about Jesus as the man who seemingly couldn't save himself but who saved others.[98] Reading the accounts of Jesus' life, it is striking how many people in terrible situations he saved. We are told that he healed the sick, raised the dead and set the oppressed free. Yet he was unable to save himself from execution.

---

94. Matthew 1:21.
95. Titus 3:5.
96. 1 Corinthians 1:18.
97. Romans 10:13.
98. Matthew 27:41, 42; D. A. Carson, *Scandalous: the cross and resurrection of Jesus* (InterVarsity Press, 2010).

Humanly speaking, that doesn't make him a very impressive Saviour! Certainly to most of those watching on that day, he was a massive disappointment. People jeered, 'If you are the Christ, come down from the cross and we will believe in you.' We are about to see how wrong they were. As someone once said, 'It is precisely because he didn't come down from the cross that we believe in him and love him.'[99]

The rebuke

Philip Greenslade recounts the story of Karl Barth, a German theologian who, on a visit to Basel prison on Good Friday in 1957, referred to this incident from Luke's Gospel when he said, 'Which is more amazing, to find Jesus in such bad company, or to find criminals in such good company?'[100] Clearly, being alongside Jesus had a profound impact on one of the two criminals being executed because, out of the blue, we find that a remarkable change had taken place in his heart.

It seems he began to experience the probe of conscience as eternity loomed in front of him while his erstwhile companion-in-crime continued his barrage. This man broke ranks and rebuked his former 'friend'. 'Do you not fear God?'[101] As we have seen earlier, God is holy and his kingdom is based on righteousness and justice.[102] The Bible warns us that it is a dreadful thing to fall into the hands of the living God.[103] Reverence and awe are the only appropriate response of

---

99. Attributed to William Booth (Salvation Army).
100. Philip Greenslade, *Voice from the Hills*, p.135, quoting Karl Barth, *Deliverance to the Captives* (SCM Press, 2012 [first published 1961]).
101. Luke 23:40 [Revised Standard Version].
102. Psalm 89:14.
103. Hebrews 10:31.

created beings before their Creator. This thief became aware of the greatness and holiness of Almighty God. The fear of God came over him.

I have never forgotten the first time I experienced something of the holiness of God. We were at a church youth group retreat. The weekend had not been going well. The behaviour of the young people had left a lot to be desired – and I was one of the leaders! On the Sunday morning, during a time of worship, someone read a passage from Isaiah about the holiness of God.[104] It is difficult to explain what happened next. Suddenly God's presence was tangible. Everyone was immediately aware of the holiness of God. Literally within a few minutes hard hearts melted and destinies were changed. This one man had a similar encounter on the cross.

Most of us continue to profess our innocence to the end or blame someone else. I've done both. In the 1994 film *The Shawshank Redemption*, Red played by Morgan Freeman is asked if he's innocent of the murder for which he's in Shawshank. He wryly observes that he's the only guilty man there. Honesty like this is unusual. Much to the surprise of everyone watching on, the thief on the cross declared his guilt and announced he was getting his just deserts. He didn't make excuses, blame others or claim extenuating circumstances. He took responsibility for his own actions. Like David in the psalms, he recognised that his sin was first and foremost against God.[105] In the same breath he acknowledged that Jesus had done nothing wrong.[106] While he was hanging next to Jesus, it seems that a seed of hope had been sown in his heart. He began to dream that there might yet be a way home.

---

104. Isaiah 6:1-8.
105. Psalm 51:4.
106. 2 Corinthians 5:21; Hebrews 4:15.

How did this happen? Jesus said nothing to him. What brought about this change? Faith is based on facts, but only comes from a personal encounter with Jesus Christ. All it took for this thief was a look. Let me explain what I mean. A couple of years earlier, the Apostle John tells us that Jesus had a night-time meeting with a member of the Jewish ruling council. The man's name was Nicodemus (we will meet him again briefly later). He was struggling to get his head around what Jesus meant when he told him that he must be born again.[107] Jesus then said something which seemed very strange: 'Just as Moses lifted up the snake in the desert, so the Son of Man must be lifted up, that everyone who believes in him may have eternal life.'[108] What on earth did he mean?

The Old Testament story Jesus was alluding to followed an incident when God's people had grumbled against him. They were being punished for their rebelliousness.[109] God sent poisonous snakes among them. In our politically correct world, we don't like anything that speaks of judgement and punishment. As a result, we miss the fact that God provided them with a way out of their predicament. Moses was told to hold up a bronze snake on a pole. Anyone who had been bitten just had to look at the snake and they would live. All it needed was one look to be saved. One look of faith. Sadly, it seems that some refused to do something so simple, and died. Hard-heartedness is a dangerous thing.

Why did they have to look at a bronze snake? My only conclusion is that it was because it would involve them acknowledging their personal sin and rebellion against God.

---
107. John 3:3, 4.
108. John 3:14, 15.
109. Numbers 21:4-9.

Jesus told Nicodemus that he would be lifted up in the same way. He was referring to the cross. Everyone who looks to him as he is lifted up and acknowledges their sin and their need of a Saviour will be saved. This is the miracle that happened for this guilty thief. Moments later and it would have been too late. One look of faith was sufficient. Many had seen Jesus raise the dead but had refused to believe. This criminal saw Jesus being put to death and believed.

The request

Here we see the evidence of this man's new-found faith. He cried out to Jesus. Crying out for help is one thing but, as we all know, everything depends on who you cry out to. Richard Pryor, the successful actor and comedian, when involved in a life-threatening car accident in 1980, realised all his money counted for nothing and all he could do was to call out to God.[110] In the book of Genesis we read of Joseph in prison in Egypt. He was innocent of all charges. He helped a fellow prisoner who just happened to be Pharaoh's cupbearer. The cupbearer was about to be released and promised Joseph he would put in a good word for him with Pharaoh. He forgot.[111] The cupbearer couldn't be relied on and Joseph was left to languish in prison.[112] This thief, however, found Jesus reliable. He simply called out, 'Jesus'. The use of Jesus' personal name by people is extremely unusual in Luke's Gospel.[113] Luke seems

---
110. Richard Pryor on the Johnny Carson Show.
111. Genesis 40:14, 23.
112. Genesis 41:1.
113. Here are the other two instances where this happens: Luke 17:13; 18:38.

to be drawing our attention to this fact. The thief may not have known Jesus beforehand but in his last moments he called out to the only person who could help him.[114]

I often think about my mother. I have many precious memories of her but what shone most brightly was her love for God and her family. At my lowest moments she just kept on loving me and praying for me. I will always be grateful to God for her. Her death from cancer in 2008 was a bitter pill to swallow. In the days before she died, close family members, including for a short time her elderly mother (my grandmother), kept a vigil around the bedside in the hospice. Eventually, my mother slipped into unconsciousness. During the hours that followed there were times when we sat quietly, lost in our own memories. There were also moments of tears and laughter as we reminisced about my mum. My grandmother was in her nineties and struggling with severe short-term memory loss. Nothing can prepare a parent for the death of their child. It's outside of the natural order of things. Watching my grandmother's outpouring of grief as she realised that her daughter was dying was heartbreaking. To see her so quickly forget and then watch the whole scenario being replayed a few minutes later was unbearable. Not being remembered is distressing. Fortunately, I don't think my mother was aware of what was happening. But even if she was aware, I know she was relying on Jesus, the one person who she knew would always remember her.

The thief's cry was bold: 'Remember me when you come into your kingdom.' 'Remember me' is the cry of anguish from many a desperate soul throughout the Bible. Hannah,

---

114. Acts 4:12.

a barren and humiliated wife.[115] Samson, a failed, flawed and ruined leader.[116] Nehemiah, who had risked everything to do something for God and yet struggled against indifference and intense opposition.[117] Job, in his darkest moment of intense physical and emotional suffering.[118] David, the God-appointed leader that people were trying to undermine.[119] Jeremiah, who'd been persecuted for speaking out for God.[120] The list goes on. If the list doesn't already include us, it could. Without exception, God will hear our cry: 'Remember me, O Lord.'[121]

This thief had come to a place of faith. He wasn't a drowning man clutching at straws. He was now convinced that Jesus was the Messiah. How did this happen? Who can understand what goes on in the heart of a person in their last moments! Someone once said to me that God looks for the first turnings in men's hearts. I remember a lady coming to church and telling us that, until recently, she had never believed in the existence of God. Then, one day, as she was driving through the village she suddenly knew there was a God. It was unexplainable to anyone else, including her husband. However, from that moment everything changed. In the ensuing weeks she was baptised into Jesus as a sign of her new-found faith. Likewise, this thief suddenly knew Jesus was who he said he was. Jesus was the Messiah who was about to enter his kingdom and this thief didn't want to be left behind.

---

115. 1 Samuel 1:11.
116. Judges 16:28.
117. Nehemiah 5:19.
118. Job 14:13, 14.
119. Psalm 25:6.
120. Jeremiah 15:15.
121. Psalm 106:4.

The response

I had lived in and worked around Southampton for 20 or so years. I was married in Old Bursledon. My children went to school in Hamble-le-Rice. Yet home was always Wales. Actually it was in Sketty, Swansea. As a family, we regularly went 'home', happily putting up with the extortionate toll charges and rain clouds at the Severn Bridge. In Welsh, there is a word for this longing, 'hiraeth'. It doesn't translate easily into English. 'Hiraeth' conveys a deep-seated desire to go home. Just before Christmas 2008 my daughter and I were 'going home'. It was a few weeks following my mother's funeral. It was a sad time. Yet, when we got there, something was different. Even though the house was the same, I left knowing it was no longer home. At that moment I realised that home was not a place, it was a person.

Jesus didn't respond to any of the derision aimed at him that day but he could not keep quiet when he heard the genuine heart cry of the dying thief. Everyone else would soon forget this man but Jesus wouldn't. The thief simply asked to be remembered. Jesus went far beyond what he asked for. 'Today you will be with me in paradise.' Hours earlier he'd been on a fast track to judgement, yet Jesus promised him that in a few moments he would be home with him in heaven, safe forever. This is Jesus' promise to all who put their trust in him.[122]

We live in a world where promises are lightly made and easily broken. Yet we can be confident of this, that Jesus always keeps his promises.[123] God loves us so much he wants us to be with him for eternity. Jesus was going home to prepare a place for all who put their trust in him.[124] Jesus was fulfilling his

---
122. 1 Thessalonians 4:17; Philippians 1:23; 2 Corinthians 5:8.
123. Hebrews 6:18-20.
124. John 14:1-4.

Father's great redemptive plan and the only way he could save us was by not saving himself!

For the thief, the doorway of heaven was now open. Paradise was beckoning. The word 'paradise' has its root in the Persian language. It referred to a walled garden, rather like the secret garden that the novelist Frances Hodgson Burnett once wrote about. All those who put their trust in what Jesus accomplished on the cross will find that the door is now open to this 'secret garden'. Jesus is both the way in[125] and the gate or door.[126] No one could come to his Father except through him. Jesus was going home to be with his Father and was going to prepare a place for us. In the Old Testament, Abraham's grandson, Jacob, was a liar and a cheat. He was not a likeable character. Yet God didn't write him off. One dark night he had an encounter with God. Jacob the crook found a stairway to heaven in the most unlikely of places.[127] Here at the cross all repentant sinners find the same!

We all hope that death is not the end. There is something within all of us that longs for heaven. As we come to a close, I want to leave you with a quote from the Christian apologist C. S. Lewis:

> *There have been times when I think we do not desire heaven; but more often I find myself wondering whether, in our heart of hearts, we have ever desired anything else ... It is the secret signature of each soul, the incommunicable and unappeasable want, the thing we desired before we met our*

---
125. John 14:6.
126. John 10:7, 9.
127. Genesis 28:12.

> *wives or made our friends or chose our work, and which we shall still desire on our deathbeds, when the mind no longer knows wife or friend or work …All your life an unattainable ecstasy has hovered just beyond the grasp of your consciousness. The day is coming when you will wake to find, beyond all hope, that you have attained it.*[128]

The result

There was no difference between the two thieves as they faced their last moments on earth. Each desperately needed forgiveness. Both had nothing going for them. Neither could save themselves. They had the same opportunity to call out to Christ. Only one did.

Today, there are still those who mock and ridicule Jesus and those who repent and trust him. I am not the first and I won't be the last to say that this incident is the only case of a death-bed conversion recorded in the Bible. There is just one, so that no one loses hope. There is just one, so that no one takes it for granted. In a graceless world that writes off many people as being beyond redemption, it is good to be reminded that not one of us is without hope. A convicted thief was the first man home!

---

128. C. S. Lewis, *The Problem of Pain* (Fontana, 1957), p.133.

CHAPTER 4

A NEW COMMUNITY

'Level Ground'

> *When the soldiers had crucified Jesus, they took his garments and divided them into four parts, one part for each soldier; also his tunic. But the tunic was seamless, woven in one piece from top to bottom, so they said to one another, 'Let us not tear it, but cast lots for it to see whose it shall be.' This was to fulfil the Scripture which says, 'They divided my garments among them, and for my clothing they cast lots.' So the soldiers did these things, but standing by the cross of Jesus were his mother and his mother's sister, Mary the wife of Clopas, and Mary Magdalene. When Jesus saw his mother and the disciple whom he loved standing nearby, he said to his mother, 'Woman, behold, your son!' Then he said to the disciple, 'Behold, your mother!' And from that hour the disciple took her to his own home.*
>
> (John 19:23-27, English Standard Version)

Coca-Cola is not the solution to world peace. None of us ever really believed it was but the company came up with a very clever piece of marketing. The culmination of the 1971 'Buy the world a Coke' advert showed young people from all over the world singing on an Italian hilltop. The message was that harmonious global unity was now achievable. Coke was 'the real thing'. Robert Woodruff, a previous company president, apparently made it his goal that no one should die without the opportunity to taste Coke. A company employee recently told me that there are only two countries where it is still not possible to buy Coca-Cola: Cuba and North Korea. Great news, world peace is just round the corner! Well, maybe not...

It was the poet John Donne who wrote, 'No man is an island.'[129] We all want to belong, be loved and be accepted. However, despite the energy we put into sharing and enjoying life with those we live amongst, for many of us genuine community is elusive. In 1988 I left Swansea and all my family and friends, and moved to South Hampshire. I had no real idea what I was looking for but I was searching for something. Looking back, I realise that I was dissatisfied with my experience of church. I also now appreciate that I was part of the problem. Reading about the early Church in action in the New Testament had only served to provoke my discontent. Having relocated, I joined a small church on the outskirts of Southampton. I added to what was already an eclectic mix of people. I fell in love with Annie and we both fell in love with the local church. God began to knit us together into a thriving and growing community. Over the years, as the church flourished, a desire for community provoked many to put their personal faith in Jesus. I still remember the night a good friend invited one of her neighbours to join a crowd of us who were going bowling. The thing that impacted her neighbour most was the sense of community that she experienced that night. As a consequence, she started coming along to our Sunday gatherings before finding a personal faith of her own. The rest is history.

At first glance, it might seem that this has little relevance to what Jesus is addressing in this his third cry from the cross. Far from it. Jesus is setting out his blueprint for a new community. These few words to his mother, Mary, and John follow on from what he has just said to one of the thieves on the cross. The

---

129. John Donne, 'Meditation XVII', *Devotions upon Emergent Occasions*, 1624.

thief had just asked Jesus to remember him when he came into his kingdom. Jesus went way beyond what he had asked for and told him that later that day he would be *with him* in paradise. Jesus was, and still is, committed to building relationship.

Created for community

Everything Jesus did in the three years prior to this day involved building community. People flocked to listen to him. They'd never heard anyone teach like this man.[130] He began to teach them the values that should underpin their relationships. It seemed so simple and yet so hard to do. Love God with all your heart and love your neighbour as yourself.[131] Jesus intentionally gathered around himself a core group of twelve disciples. For three years they travelled together and shared life. The number of Jesus' followers grew. When some found Jesus' teaching too challenging and drifted away, the twelve stayed. They had left everything to follow Jesus.[132] They seemed 'all in'.

Each of us has an inner desire for community. This should not come as a surprise. God has placed it in us. To understand why, we need to briefly delve into what the Bible teaches. Right at the beginning of the Bible, in the book of Genesis, there are hints of what Christians have traditionally referred to as the Trinity.[133] One God[134] yet three persons: God the Father, God the Son and God the Holy Spirit.[135] Each has a distinct role whilst all remain equally God. Paul, when writing to

---
130. Matthew 7:28.
131. Matthew 22:37-39.
132. Luke 18:28; see also John 6:66-68.
133. Genesis 1:26: 'Let us make man in our image, in our likeness . . .'
134. Ephesians 4:6.
135. 2 Corinthians 13:14.

the church in Ephesus, describes something of how they work together: 'For through him [Jesus] we both have access to the Father by one Spirit.'[136] This is a great mystery.

In the book of Exodus, when Moses wants to know the name of God he is told, 'I am who I am' has been speaking to him.[137] At first glance it seems a strange name. Yet God's name is always 'I am' because there is no past or present with him. He is eternal. God the Father has always been the Father because Jesus has always been the Son. God (Father, Son and Spirit) exists in perfect community.[138]

It is important that we understand that God didn't create human beings because he was lacking in some way. God was not lonely and didn't need friends. He didn't need someone to love. He is love.[139] The truth is that love can only be expressed in community. I can only be loving when there is someone to love. So if God is love he must exist in community. However, because God is love he wanted to create a bigger family. This is why he created us in his image. This is why we are made for community.

God also knew that Adam needed human companionship. We are told that it was not good for him to be alone.[140] So God created Eve. She was to be Adam's helper. Interestingly, the same word is used of God when the Bible says that he is our helper. God-created community must have a focus and that focus should always be God himself. We first see this in the Garden of Eden where God loved to walk with Adam and Eve in the cool of the evening.[141] Community is central to God's plans.

---

136. Ephesians 2:18.
137. Exodus 3:14.
138. Michael Reeves' *The Good God: Enjoying Father, Son and Spirit* (Paternoster, 2012) is an excellent book to read if you want to study this in more depth.
139. 1 John 4:16.
140. Genesis 2:18.
141. Genesis 3:8.

Crushing of community

Crucifixion was a tool used by the Romans to destroy community. It was far more than just a means of execution for hardened criminals. There were quicker and easier ways of killing people. It was a way of imposing their authority by publicly instilling terror. It ensured that Roman rule was far less likely to be challenged. In effect, it was a brutal form of crowd control. More specifically, the Jewish religious leaders were using the cross as a way of finally crushing Jesus' community of followers. The night before his arrest, Jesus had been on the Mount of Olives with his disciples. He had previously warned them they would all abandon him.[142] As he faced the horror of what he knew lay in front of him, he needed comfort. He turned to his Father in prayer. He also wanted his closest friends to stand with him as he prayed.[143] They fell asleep. So much for his friends! By the next day, pretty much all of Jesus' disciples had fled. Left in front of the cross was a small group of people – predominantly women – watching the end of all their hopes and dreams.

From the beginning of the Bible, the devil has sought to destroy God's community and replace it with a parody of the real thing. Like Frankenstein's monster, it might have most of the right bits stitched together but it doesn't have God's heart. God created us to live and flourish together with him. In the middle of his garden was a tree. The tree of the knowledge of good and evil.[144] God gave Adam permission to eat of any tree in the garden except that one. It was God's garden. It was God's way of ensuring that Adam put him first. The devil first

---
142. Mark 14:27.
143. Matthew 26:36-45.
144. Genesis 2:17.

deceived Eve before Adam knowingly ate from the tree. Adam failed to keep God at the centre of his life. Adam's sin caused a chasm between God and man. Ever since that day, God planned for Jesus to come and restore the broken relationship. This is why, at the cross, the devil was desperate to put the final nails in the coffin of God's community.

Since Adam's rebellion, we too have all ignored God and continued to pursue our attempts to create a community of our own making. From the Tower of Babel through to the twenty-first century we have sought to establish a society without reference to God. All our efforts are doomed because of the self-focus and self-sufficiency that are deeply rooted in the human heart. Sin corrupts community. Society's problems will never be solved by politicians, academics or practitioners. The answer will not be found in a new social initiative. Until we humble ourselves and God is restored to his rightful place, there is no hope.

On the cross it may have looked like all was lost but, as far as Jesus was concerned, it was going to plan. Here God would fashion the community he always intended.

Conceiving a new community

In these few words of Jesus we find the birth of a new community. Jesus saw his mother. In his anguish, as he was being punished for our sin, he still saw the pain of others. His selflessness cuts right to the heart of our self-focused society. Mary had carried him in her own womb and given birth to the Son of God. She had cared for him as he grew up. She had lived with the prophecy of Simeon, given at his dedication. Simeon had told her that Jesus would cause national upheaval. He had also said, enigmatically, that a sword would pierce her own heart.[145] Now, in front of the cross, Mary understood. She could feel the stabbing pain of it as she helplessly watched on. Marcus Loane poignantly draws our attention to the depth of this pain. He reminds us that the same woman, who experienced such joy at the birth of a son, now experienced inconsolable grief as she watched him die.[146]

Here we see the compassion of the cross. Jesus deliberately did not use the term 'mother', now or at any other point, when talking to Mary. To our ears it may seem harsh but 'woman' was a term of tenderness and respect.[147] Whilst he loved Mary, his language carried an edge of restraint. It is clear that Jesus' flesh-and-blood ties did not have the importance that we would attach to them.[148] I don't think that Mary would have been surprised because she knew that he was always about his Father's business.[149] We are also reminded of Jesus' love for John. All his disciples had fled;[150] only one returned, 'the disciple whom he loved'.

Virtually all commentators believe that this was John himself.

To the very last, Jesus was focused on others. Here is a great truth, that when he was on the cross, we were on his mind. It was for the joy set before him that he endured the cross, scorning its shame.[151] The joy set before him was that he would, as a result of what he suffered, be able to bring many sons and daughters to his Father.[152] The nineteenth-

---

145. Luke 2:34, 35.
146. Marcus Loane, *The Voice of the Cross*, p.48.
147. John 2:4.
148. Matthew 12:46-50.
149. Luke 2:49.
150. Matthew 26:56.
151. Hebrews 12:2.
152. Hebrews 2:10.

century Bishop of Liverpool, J. C. Ryle, wrote: 'The heart that even on the cross felt for Mary, is a heart that never changes. Jesus never forgets any who love him, and even in their worst estate remembers their need. No wonder that Peter says, "Cast all your care upon him; for he cares for you."' [153] At the cross, we see the compassionate heart of God towards men and women.

Jesus would, by now, have been weak from the loss of blood, dehydration, the heat of the near-eastern sun and the emotional and mental agony of what he was going through. It therefore comes as a complete surprise to find him issuing an order. 'Behold'[154] was a word of command. John used it several times in his Gospel and it always carried a tone of authority: 'Behold, the Lamb of God, who takes away the sin of the world!'[155] 'Behold the man!'[156] 'Behold your King!'[157] Jesus clearly wanted their attention. Similarly, he wants our attention! Look and listen because what he is about to say is still of profound importance.

Yet, at first reading, what Jesus actually said feels like an anti-climax. To Mary he said that John is now going to be your son, and vice versa. Is that all? What is all the fuss about?

The challenge of this new community

In fact, Jesus' words are deeply challenging. Until now, Jesus had been responsible for his mother. It appears that Joseph had died some time previously. There is no reference to him after Jesus

---

153. J. C. Ryle, *Expository Thoughts on the Gospels*: John, p.331.
154. Greek 'ide'.
155. John 1:29 [English Standard Version].
156. John 19:5 [English Standard Version].
157. John 19:14 [English Standard Version].

was 12 years old. It seems probable that Jesus had worked for years as a carpenter in Nazareth to provide for the family.[158] First and foremost, there can be no doubt that the commandment to honour his father and mother was something Jesus took very seriously.[159] Even on the cross Jesus fulfilled the law.

When my mother died, my stepfather, whom I was very fond of, continued to live in the family home. Her death, perhaps not unexpectedly, had an impact relationally. My stepfather had his own children. Even though my sister and I were, and still are, good friends with them, my mother's death had an impact on the dynamics of our relationship. They understandably felt an obligation to look after their father. We had to try to be careful that we didn't overstep our responsibilities. Relationships are complicated.

Jesus, however, drove a truck through the social etiquette of the day. 'Mary, this is your son. John, here is your mother.' John obeyed Jesus and thereafter treated Mary as his own mother. But what about Jesus' brothers and sisters (of course they were actually his half-brothers and half-sisters)?[160] Mary was their mother too and also their responsibility. What on earth would they have thought? Was Jesus saying that his brothers and sisters were not fit to look after their mother? There is no evidence that this was the case. In fact, Jesus' brothers seem to have had a close relationship with their mother. We read of them all coming to challenge Jesus because of the family concern over what they considered was his crazy schedule.[161] What about John's mother? How would she have felt? What

---

158. Mark 6:3.
159. Exodus 20:12.
160. Mark 6:3.
161. Mark 3:21, 31.

about Zebedee, John's father? First of all, Jesus had taken his two sons away from the family business[162] and then Jesus dropped Mary like a cuckoo into the family nest . . . I'm sure that he would have been more gracious than this! Yet what did Zebedee make of it all?

Jesus did not deliberately set out to cause problems within established families, although he knew that this would inevitably happen.[163] Rather, he was determined to create a new community that was not based on human values. This would be the restoration of God's new community that would continue beyond the grave.

The crux of what Jesus was doing was putting right Adam's sin. At the tree in God's garden, Adam allowed self-centredness to ruin the community God had created. His sin was inherited by every man and woman,[164] with the exception of Jesus.[165] Jesus, who Paul later calls the last Adam,[166] bore our sin on his body on the tree.[167] Jesus, the last Adam, did what the first Adam should have done. He refused 'self' and willingly submitted to his Father's plan. Jesus became a curse to break the curse.[168] The result is a restoration of the community God always intended.

Cross-shaped community

Here at the cross, as Jesus hung between heaven and earth, he was reconciling man to God. Here at the cross, as Jesus' arms were stretched to breaking point, he was reaching out

---

162. Mark 1:19, 20.
163. Luke 12:51-53.
164. Romans 5:12.
165. Hebrews 4:15.
166. 1 Corinthians 15:45.
167. 1 Peter 2:24.
168. Galatians 3:13.

THROUGH

'Between Heaven and Earth'

to all people. Here at the cross, God's new community was established. The early Church sought to embody all that Christ had accomplished and their corporate love for him engendered a powerful sense of belonging. Their life together, while not perfect, stood out in a world that was as materialistic and self-indulgent as ours. It was their radical commitment to work out Jesus' teaching to love their neighbour as themselves that resulted in the basic provision of social security.[169] The way they lived attracted widespread attention and caused many to come to trust in Jesus.

This is community based on faith in Christ. There is no entrance exam to pass – which is just as well because everyone would fail. There is no membership fee to pay – which is good because no one could afford it. We don't have to be perfect to be part of this community – which means we are all eligible. God loves us completely so no one can blackball us. All we need do to belong is to humble ourselves and personally put our trust in Christ to save us. It is about us freely receiving what he has done for us. This is grace. Peter says that Jesus is the cornerstone upon which this new community is built. Every believer in Jesus is like a living stone built on the foundation of Jesus. We are a people belonging to God.[170]

Paul goes on to explain in more detail that God's people, his Church, is not based on nationality, circumcision or status but rather on Christ.[171] He says that Jesus' 'purpose was to create in himself one new man'.[172] One new man in Christ. What does this mean? It means that the Church is the body of Christ and he is the head. We are all parts of his body.[173] As such, we are

---

169. Rodney Stark, *The Rise of Christianity* (HarperOne, 1997), p.207.
170. 1 Peter 2:4-10.
171. Galatians 3:28; Colossians 3:11.
172. Ephesians 2:15.
173. 1 Corinthians 12:12-27.

all equally valued. No one can say that they are not needed or that they are unimportant. We cannot do without one another. Like a beautiful jigsaw, we 'fit together' even though we all have different roles to play. We are now to live as Jesus did by putting others before ourselves. As the novelist Alexander Dumas used as a motto for his *Three Musketeers*: 'All for one and one for all.' Being part of God's new community brings fulfilment and a sense of completeness.

Annie and I have just returned from the West Coast of America. One of the stand-out moments involved a visit to see the redwoods of Northern California. These trees are hundreds of years old and have grown to over 300 feet high in close proximity to one another. Staggeringly, their roots are only six to twelve feet deep. How have they remained standing in the midst of the Pacific storms? The answer is that each tree's roots intertwine with those around it. Their strength is in their community. Likewise, the churches that have the greatest longevity are made up of people whose 'roots' have intertwined with each other. They stand together, strengthening one another in the storms of life. Their closeness to one another helps them grow straight in the same direction so they become more like Christ. They are committed to where God has planted them and the people that he has put them amongst. They are less concerned about their own visibility and role than they are about the church or, as Paul calls it, the body. This commitment is driven, first and foremost, by their love for God and then their love for one another. Such people make any church leader's work a joy.[174]

The community of the cross is powerful. Together, we are more than the sum of our collective parts because God

---

174. Hebrews 13:17.

is with us. No wonder, then, that the Bible says all things are possible for us.[175] If that were not enough, it is only here that we can fully know one another. The American pastor and writer Tim Keller, unpacking a C. S. Lewis quote, says an individual is best known in community.[176] Let me explain the gist of what he means. My relationship with my daughter, Meg, gives me a greater appreciation of Simon, her husband. Meg helps me to see in Simon the amazing qualities I might otherwise miss in him.

Here, amongst God's people, the unloved can know love, the lonely can find friendship and the destitute can be cared for. Jesus is so closely associated with his new community that if we hurt his people we hurt him[177] and that if we care for them we care for him.[178] The example of this new community, Jesus' Church, should convince everyone of the power of the gospel and provoke people around us to believe in Jesus.[179] The Church is a group of imperfect people who have received the grace of God and in doing so found life together with Christ. The American Christian author Philip Yancey points out that we are a community hungry for grace. Like addicts on a recovery course, we share the same weakness. When we convince ourselves that we can make it on our own, grace breaks in to rectify our foolishness.[180]

Over many years I've watched as people from all sorts of backgrounds become followers of Jesus. Yet the church hasn't

---

175. Romans 8:31.
176. Tim Keller, *The Prodigal God* (Hodder & Stoughton, 2009), pp.126-7, quoting from C. S. Lewis, *The Weight of Glory and other addresses* (SPCK, 1942), who is talking about the death of a friend, Charles Williams.
177. Acts 9:5.
178. Matthew 25:31-46.
179. John 17:22, 23.
180. *What's so Amazing about Grace?* (Zondervan, 1998), p.273.

turned into a melting pot where people simply coexist. A far more profound change has occurred. At the foot of the cross we embrace a completely new identity. We're no longer defined by our ethnicity, gender or sexuality. Our identity is now in Christ. Our defining differences disappear as we die to our old life and embrace the new life Jesus offers. Quite literally we become new creations. The old has gone, the new has come.[181] Our new identity shapes our behaviour. We now want to please Jesus. We may come as we are but we never stay as we are. There is nothing on earth like being part of his loving grace-filled community.

There is a day coming when God's new community will finally be complete. We will spend eternity with Jesus, fully enjoying all that God has created and sharing life with those we already know in Christ and those we don't yet know.

At the foot of the cross is level ground and there is room for all.

---

181. 2 Corinthians 5:17.

CHAPTER 5

VICTORY THROUGH DEFEAT

'Forsaken'

> *From the sixth hour until the ninth hour darkness came over all the land. About the ninth hour, Jesus cried out in a loud voice, 'Eli, Eli, lema sabachthani?' which means, 'My God, My God, why have you forsaken Me?' When some of those standing there heard this, they said, 'He is calling Elijah.'*
>
> (Matthew 27:45-47, Berean Study Bible)

God-forsaken is not a phrase we use much today. It conveys a sense of utter desolation and abandonment. It is difficult for us to appreciate the full depth of its meaning. The people of Japan did, following the events of 6 August 1945. An American plane, a B29 bomber named 'Enola Gay' after the pilot's mother, flew over the city of Hiroshima. The plane was carrying an atomic bomb. The war between America and Japan was about to be brought to a swift and devastating conclusion. At around 8.15 in the morning, Japanese time, the bomb was detonated 2,000 feet above the city. The immediate explosion destroyed around ninety per cent of Hiroshima, levelling an area with a radius of two and a half kilometres. An estimated 80,000 people were killed in the blast with a further 60,000 dying of their injuries and radiation-related causes in the following 5 years. God-forsaken was an apt description of the scene that met the eyes of the waking world that morning. Not too many events through history warrant the use of such an epithet, although another one that does is recorded for us in Matthew's Gospel.

The bleak cry from the lips of Jesus conveyed that he knew what it was like to have been forsaken and abandoned by God the Father. His first three cries from the cross were associated with the needs of others. In the coming chapters we'll see that the last three cries were more personal. This, the fourth cry, stands alone: 'My God, my God, why have you forsaken me?' Matthew tells us that Jesus used just four words in Aramaic. We will find that the depths of agony behind these four stark words are impossible for us to fully comprehend. Even though the loudness of the cry was a sign of his anguish, this was no dying 'Braveheart shout' for the crowd. This was Jesus, the Son of God, fulfilling his Father's will. As we sense Jesus' horror at being forsaken, it is easy to wrongly conclude that what happened on the cross was a crushing defeat. However, what looked like defeat would pave the way for ultimate victory.

Lost intimacy

I vividly remember my mother telling me of her panic when she thought she had lost me when I was four years old. The baker left the back gate open and I seized the opportunity to make a run for it. I was brought back into 'custody' an hour or two later, having been found walking along the main road heading out of the village. Funnily enough, the first time we read of Jesus, after the events surrounding his remarkable birth, is after he has gone missing for three days! His parents had thought that their 12-year-old boy was with someone else in their group as they made the journey home from their annual trip to Jerusalem. In fact, Jesus was still in the Temple talking with the religious teachers. The people who listened to him were amazed at his understanding and answers. A day passed by before his parents realised that he was missing and it was three days before they found him. This would be every parent's worst nightmare. On finding him, his mother told him off: 'Son, why have you treated us like this? Your father and I have been anxiously searching for you.' Jesus' reply was startling: 'Didn't you know I had to be in my Father's house?'[182] Right from the beginning Jesus talked about God being his Father. This only makes sense if what we considered about the Trinity in the last chapter is true. God the Father always has been, always is, and always will be the Father. Likewise, Jesus was and always will be the Son.

On more than 20 occasions, the Gospels record Jesus praying to God. Every time, bar this one, he called God, 'Father'.[183] He even taught his disciples to do the same. He told people that he was always about his Father's business.[184] This meant that he only ever did what he saw him doing[185] and only ever said what he heard him saying.[186] The Gospels make it clear that Jesus knew that his Father loved him[187] and he only did what pleased his Father.[188] On the night prior to his arrest, knowing the agony that lay ahead of him, Jesus needed to spend time with his Father in prayer. In his anguish his only comfort was that he knew he was doing his Father's will.[189]

In front of us is the only time when Jesus' intimate relationship with his Father was broken. As he took our place and bore our sin, he was unable to call God, Father. Jesus experienced the horror of what it was to be separated from God. His Father couldn't look upon our sin, and turned his face away. As the Old Testament prophet Habakkuk explained, God's 'eyes are too pure to look on evil'.[190] We will never fully comprehend the cost of the cross. And Jesus did it for us.

---

182. Luke 2:41-49.
183. Matthew 6:9.
184. John 6:38.
185. John 5:19.
186. John 8:28.
187. Luke 3:22; John 5:20.
188. John 8:29.
189. Luke 22:41-44.
190. Habakkuk 1:13.

Persevering faith

The way we call out to someone conveys a lot. When I was growing up if my father shouted, 'Stephen, come here now!' it was time to head for the hills. The words that he used told me everything I needed to know. I was invariably in deep trouble. Jesus' words were telling: 'My God, my God.' Despite experiencing his Father's anger at sin, he never stopped trusting God. Jesus persevered in faith. Twice he called God, 'My God.' Repetition like this in the Bible is always for emphasis. In the bleakest of circumstances Jesus never despaired. He still knew he had a personal relationship with God despite being separated from him. This is the sort of faith that pleases God.[191] Nothing brings more honour to God than when we trust him in the face of difficult circumstances. This is what the heroes of the Bible were commended for in Hebrews. It is only possible for us to persevere in faith because of our hope in what Jesus has accomplished for us.

The cross is the central point of the gospel. If Jesus' death wasn't necessary then we can be sure that God would not have allowed his beloved Son to die. There was no tragic mistake as some would try to have us believe. In the midst of this, his final challenge, Jesus clung fiercely to God. His stark cry was a declaration of his faith amidst the absence of his Father. Those who heard him would have recognised that he was quoting directly from the psalms.[192] David, the author, had written these words as an anguished cry for God's help when he was suffering a prolonged personal attack. This psalm has remarkable similarities with what Jesus experienced on the cross. We will look at this in more detail in a moment.

---

191. Hebrews 11:6.
192. Psalm 22:1.

A rhetorical question

Watching the news unfold in the media we cannot avoid seeing terrible injustices being committed alongside horrific cruelty to fellow human beings. It can leave us asking ourselves the question, 'Where is God in all of this?' In such moments, 'Why?' is never far from our lips. In 1993 a change in the law meant it was possible for religious groups to advertise on television. The Guardian newspaper invited five advertising agencies to put together campaigns to seek to address the decline in Church of England congregations. One of the advertising agencies proposed a campaign homing in on human suffering. Their suggested campaign headline ran 'Why Hillsborough? Why Bosnia? Why Zeebrugge? God only knows.' All of us struggle with these sorts of questions. It helps us to know that Jesus himself asked: 'Why?'[193]

Having said that, it is important that we understand that Jesus was not questioning God's integrity. Jesus already knew the answer. His was a rhetorical question. This is not the first time we come across Jesus doing this. In the place called Gethsemane, when the mob came to arrest him, he asked them who they were looking for. He did so knowing they had come to arrest him.[194] All of us do something similar to this from time to time. Usually I do it loudly in order to show my irritation. 'Who left this handbag on the stairs? – I could have broken my neck!' I already know whose bag it is. There are only two of us living in the house and I don't own a handbag! By loudly raising the question I am expressing my frustration, hoping that the

---

193. The *Guardian Weekend* magazine, 10 April 1993, 'Selling God', p.11. Courtesy of Guardian News & Media Ltd.
194. John 18:4.

guilty party is listening. Sometimes I even do it when she is not in the house!

Jesus was not questioning God. Rather, by his question he was expressing something of the horror of what he was going through. He had known that he would be forsaken by his closest disciples and friends but when that happened he was comforted by still having his Father's presence with him. As he had told them, 'You will leave me all alone. Yet I am not alone, for my Father is with me.'[195] However, he always knew that the moment would come when he would be left by his Father. There is no doubt this was in the forefront of his mind on the Mount of Olives the night before his crucifixion. We are told by Luke that the mental anguish and distress were so great that he sweated what were like drops of blood.[196] Medically speaking, it is possible that it was blood. It can happen when someone is under extreme duress (it is known as 'haematidrosis'). Despite the extent of his suffering, Jesus knew the answer to his question. The Gospels tell us that Jesus knew the reason why he would suffer on the cross.

He knew he had come to rescue people

Matthew tells us that in the three hours in the middle of the day there was complete darkness. We all know what it is to have nightmares and a few of us have experienced night terrors. Darkness has the effect of making everything seem much worse! On the cross, in what was supposed to be the brightest part of the day, the darkness only served to heighten Jesus' anguish.

---
195. John 16:32.
196. Luke 22:44.

Yet there is a deeper meaning. Throughout the Bible 'darkness' is used to speak of our sin which has separated us from God, who is light.[197] Isaiah had prophesied about Jesus' birth centuries earlier when he said that the people living in darkness would see a great light.[198] We all know that when we are in the dark it is difficult to appreciate just how dark it is until we put the light on. John describes Jesus' incarnation as light coming into darkness.[199] His arrival on planet Earth exposed the full extent of the darkness in our hearts.[200] Jesus knew that he had come to rescue people who were lost in darkness, far from God.[201]

He knew that he had come to resolve our problem

Jesus was never in any doubt that human beings loved darkness rather than light. This is true of every person who has ever lived, with the sole exception of Jesus himself. The Bible has a word for the solution: propitiation.[202] It is not a popular word in some church circles today. However, just because people don't like it doesn't mean it isn't true. Propitiation requires that God's righteous anger at our sin must be appeased if we are going to be restored into relationship with him. It involves more than just our sin being forgiven. Forgiveness can be received only if God's wrath is appeased. The deep darkness of these moments on the cross conveyed that Jesus, as he bore the burden of our sin, was being exposed to the wrath of a just and holy God. Jesus knew that Isaiah had prophesied centuries earlier that this

---

197. 1 John 1:5.
198. Isaiah 9:2.
199. John 1:1-5.
200. In John 8:12 Jesus calls himself the 'light of the world'.
201. Luke 19:10.
202. Hebrews 2:17.

would happen.[203] There was something about Jesus' cry which, although brutally honest, rings true and gives us confidence that Jesus has paid our debt before God once and for all.[204] John Calvin, the sixteenth-century French theologian, simply said that Jesus bore in his soul 'the tortures of condemned and ruined man'.[205]

He knew that he had come to restore our relationship with his Father

Jesus was clear that, because of his death on the cross, he would bring many sons to God.[206] It explains his confidence in promising the thief alongside him that he would, that day, be with him in paradise. It was for the joy of seeing this accomplished that he persevered and put up with the shame.[207] Paul, when writing to the Corinthian church, explains what really happened on that day: 'For God made Christ, who never sinned, to be the offering for our sin, so that we could be made right with God through Christ.'[208]

God-forsaken

In these dark moments, Jesus still knew that God loved him. He still knew that God's Spirit was with him. Jesus never ceased being part of the Trinity. Irrespective of all this, nothing could have prepared him for what he experienced in those

---

203. Isaiah 53:5, 6, 10.
204. William Lane, *The Gospel of Mark* (William B. Eerdmans, 1995), p.573.
205. John Calvin, *Institutes* II:XVI, 10. Available at http://www.ntslibrary.com/PDF%20Books/Calvin%20Institutes%20of%20Christian%20Religion.pdf
206. Isaiah 53:11.
207. Hebrews 12:2.
208. 2 Corinthians 5:21 [New Living Translation].

hours on the cross. In truth, it is way beyond our ability to comprehend. Apparently, when contemplating this statement by Jesus, Martin Luther, the sixteenth-century theologian and reformer, spent hours lost in thought. After a long time he stood up and was heard to say, 'God forsaking God! No man can understand that.'[209]

A friend of mine takes groups – mainly men – to visit the Normandy beaches and the sites of the D-Day landings. I have had the privilege of going a couple of times. Omaha Beach was the scene for some of the fiercest fighting that day. As the US troops came ashore, they were assailed by a hail of bullets and mortar. By all accounts, the opening scenes of the film *Saving Private Ryan* give us a realistic idea of what they experienced on D-Day. The film is not for the faint-hearted. Standing on Omaha Beach in 'Dog Green Sector', it is still possible to see the machine gun bunker, one of the reasons why so many lost their lives on this part of the beach that day. Survivors talked of the harrowing sound of the dying, many of them just boys, calling out to God and their mothers and fathers. Forsaken says it all.

David wrote in one of his psalms, 'I was young and now I am old, yet I have never seen the righteous forsaken . . .'.[210] David may never have seen it but many outside Jerusalem did that day, and Matthew vividly records for us the last cry of the forsaken. Jesus genuinely experienced what it was to be abandoned, totally cut off from his Father. In these moments, Jesus encountered God not as Father but as the just and Holy One.

What happened on the cross bears extraordinary similarities with what another psalm says:

---

209. Quoted by C. H. Spurgeon, *Spurgeon at his best*, p.272.
210. Psalm 37:25.

> *My God, my God, why have you forsaken me? Why are you so far from saving me, so far from the words of my groaning?...*
>
> *All who see me mock me; they hurl insults, shaking their heads:*
>
> *'He trusts in the Lord; let the Lord rescue him. Let him deliver him, since he delights in him.'...*
>
> *I am poured out like water, and all my bones are out of joint. My heart has turned to wax; it has melted away within me. My strength is dried up like a potsherd, and my tongue sticks to the roof of my mouth...*
>
> *...a band of evil men has encircled me, they have pierced my hands and my feet. I can count all my bones; people stare and gloat over me. They divide my garments among them and cast lots for my clothing.*[211]

Jesus clearly knew this psalm. He wasn't quoting it to ensure a prophecy was fulfilled. It was only a messianic prophecy *because* Jesus fulfilled it. Under the most intense pressure, what came out of his heart was the same sentiment as the psalmist. Jesus' experience of being God-forsaken gives hope to all who feel abandoned. The sister of the twentieth-century Christian author Corrie Ten Boom, Betsy, just before she died

---

211. Psalm 22:1, 7, 8, 14, 15, 16-18.

in the Ravensbrück concentration camp, whispered to her sister, 'We must tell them that there is no pit so deep that He is not deeper still.'[212] However forsaken we may feel, Jesus has been there and understands the pain. If he has been there, the good news is he has provided the way out for us. For some, like Betsy, there is no 'happy ever after' this side of heaven. Others, though, experience a foretaste of heaven on earth when God brings them out of the pit they are in. Yet one day we will all have to cross the threshold of death and when we do we will find out that the best this world had to offer was only a pale shadow of the real thing.

I first met Joan after she had been widowed. She was distraught following her husband's death. Neither she nor her husband believed in God, or so she thought. After the funeral, she was looking through his books, one of which was a Bible. He had used it to do the cryptic crossword. On opening it, she realised it had become more than just a reference tool – he had read it. What was more shocking was that it was clear from his handwritten notes in the margins that he had become a Christian. He had never told her! Why hadn't he talked to her about it? She felt doubly forsaken. Then one night she had a vivid dream. She saw her husband, standing in a place she didn't recognise, beckoning her. At her local surgery, one of the nurses invited her to come along to the Sunday morning gathering of the church. To her shock, when she came, she recognised the auditorium as the place she had seen in her dream. In the coming weeks she too came to a personal faith in Christ and found the answer to the ache in her heart. Jesus was forsaken so that she might not be.

---

212. Corrie Ten Boom, *The Hiding Place* (Hodder & Stoughton, 2004), p.202.

Certain outcome

In November 2008 the Reverend A. Glyn Morris, then well into his nineties, conducted the committal of my mother's body at Oystermouth Cemetery, overlooking the Mumbles. This is the gist of what he said that day. 'At bleak moments like this, grammar is important. For many, this moment is followed by a full stop. This is the atheist. They are convinced this life is all there is. For others it is followed by a question mark. This is the agnostic. They are not sure whether there is anything beyond the grave or not. If there is, they hope they will be all right. For the Christian this moment is followed by a comma, because the best is yet to come!' On the cross Jesus paid for our sin. For all who put their trust in him, death is not the end. We have a sure and certain hope. Jesus knew what it was to be forsaken. Yet in the next three chapters we will see that he was not overcome with hopelessness. He was sure that God would vindicate him. The same psalm that Jesus had just quoted would have given him great assurance because it says: 'For he has not despised or disdained the suffering of the afflicted one; he has not hidden his face from him but has listened to his cry for help. From you comes the theme of my praise in the great assembly.'[213] Jesus fully expected to stand in God's presence and see this promise fulfilled. He was confident of ultimate victory despite experiencing seeming defeat.

The twentieth-century Christian writer Hubert Simpson, in his book *Testament of Love*,[214] made reference to a painting by Francis Martin. Martin had served in the Royal Engineer

---
213. Psalm 22:24, 25.
214. Hubert Simpson, *Testament of Love* (Hodder & Stoughton, 1934), p.121. The painting is also referred to by Marcus Loane in his book *The Voice of the Cross*, p.21.

Signal Service (now the Royal Corps of Signals) in World War I in Northern France. On his return from action he was commissioned to paint an incident that happened during the war. His painting showed an unarmed lineman's body, lying forsaken in no man's land. He had been sent to repair the severed communication line. In the act of completing his mission he had been fatally wounded. In his dying moments, he ensured that communications were restored. The painting was evocatively called *Through*.[215] It summarises what Jesus accomplished on the cross. Jesus, sent by his Father, crossed over into the desolation of no-man's land caused by our sin. In his dying act he ensured that the connection that had been broken between God and man was restored. Through him we can now have access to God.

When we put our trust in Jesus, in all that he is and all that he has accomplished through his death on the cross, he saves us completely. We need never fear being forsaken by God. This is why the writer of Hebrews can say with such confidence that God will never leave us or forsake us.[216] Victory through defeat has become reality.

---

215. The painting *Through* inspired the title for this book. At the time of writing it is being displayed in the Royal Corps of Signals HQ in Blandford Forum, Dorset.
216. Hebrews 13:5.

CHAPTER 6

DYING FOR A DRINK

'The Sea Is Never Full'

> *Later, knowing that all was now completed, and so that Scripture would be fulfilled, Jesus said, 'I am thirsty.' A jar of wine vinegar was there, so they soaked a sponge in it, put the sponge on a stalk of the hyssop plant, and lifted it to Jesus' lips.*
>
> (John 19:28, 29)

'I'm dying for a drink' is a phrase I occasionally use but which is never true. It brings to mind a film I first saw in my early teens, *Ice Cold in Alex*.[217] The main thread which runs through the film is the desire of Captain Anson, played by John Mills, for an ice-cold beer in Alexandria. The storyline involves a small group of nurses and soldiers crossing the North African desert in order to get back behind Allied lines in World War II. The conditions are harsh. They are on the verge of dying for a drink. The film ends with the main characters sitting in a bar in Alexandria, quenching their thirst. Have you ever been that thirsty? In truth, I haven't.

We now come to consider the fifth of Jesus' cries from the cross. It seems fairly straightforward. If we take what he said at face value he was simply asking for a drink. By now, however, I hope you realise there is always more to what Jesus said than meets the eye. These three simple words, 'I am thirsty', reflect more than just the cry of a tortured soul who has hung on a Roman cross through the heat of the day. Mind you, who of us would blame Jesus for uttering such a heartfelt cry? It is a terrible way to die. The explorer William Coulthard died of thirst in the Australian desert in 1858. When his remains were discovered three months later, they found that he had scrawled a last tortured message on to his water canteen: 'I never

---

217. *Ice Cold* in Alex made in 1958, starring John Mills, Anthony Quayle and Sylvia Syms.

reached water . . . my tung is stkig to my mouth . . . my tung burn . . . I can see no way. God help. I can't get up.'[218]

We can survive without food for weeks but only days without water. Dehydration can quickly cause the strongest person to become delirious. As soon as they are rehydrated they typically return to their senses. Our own experience tells each of us how much we need water. I live in a privileged part of the world where water is on tap 24 hours a day. Yet for all of humanity's so-called progress, thousands of people around the world are dying every day from dehydration or easily preventable diseases caused by drinking polluted water. Dying for a drink is a reality for them.

This was not what it was like right at the very beginning. God created a world with plenty of water. The garden that Adam and Eve lived in and cultivated flourished in part because it was the source of four rivers that watered the region.[219] Adam and Eve lacked for nothing. Standing behind the beauty of creation, the peace and fulfilment they enjoyed and even the food and water they needed to sustain life, was God. He was the source of all they needed. Their need of water was a daily reminder of their dependence on the God who created and sustained them.

His provision

Throughout the Bible, lack of water and drought conditions were usually signs that men and women had turned away from God.[220] The world God created has been ruined by our sin. Lack

---

218. This is a slightly shortened extract. The fuller extract can be found in David Hunt's *True Girl: The Unauthorised History of Australia*, Vol.2 (Black Inc., 2016).
219. Genesis 2:10-14.
220. Deuteronomy 28:15, 23, 24; 1 Kings 17:1.

of water, amongst other things, should be a provocation for us to seek the only one who can sustain us physically, emotionally and spiritually. In the Old Testament, God's wayward people, the children of Israel, wandered through a desert for 40 years. During this time, their need for fresh water, in what was an arid and inhospitable terrain, should have caused them to put their trust in God on a daily basis. God always intended to provide for them, yet he wanted their devotion.[221] There were moments when he specifically used their thirst to test their hearts. On one occasion he miraculously provided water from a rock when Moses struck it with his staff.[222] Instead of being grateful, they grumbled, complained and quarrelled with God and Moses. Yet despite their recalcitrance, God mercifully kept providing water for them.

How we respond to God in such moments is crucial. He is looking for people whose hearts are completely committed to him.[223] It is only our trust in him that pleases God.[224] In one telling incident, towards the end of their 40 years in the wilderness, the children of Israel were still grumbling at God because of a lack of water. They simply hadn't learned the lesson. Moses showed his frustration. God told him that all he needed to do was to *speak* to the rock and God would provide water. Instead Moses struck the rock with his staff, just as he had done previously.[225] God still caused water to pour out, despite Moses not having trusted God. We will see later that his disobedience was to cost him dear.

---

221. Exodus 15:27.
222. Exodus 17:1-7.
223. 2 Chronicles 16:9.
224. Hebrews 11:6.
225. Numbers 20:1-13.

The challenge we all face is to trust God when we are in the most difficult of circumstances. With this in mind, let's see how Jesus responded at the height of his trial.

His test

It was approaching the ninth hour, around three o'clock in the afternoon. Jesus had already been on the cross for six hours.[226] The combination of blood loss, exhaustion, nervous tension and exposure to the searing midday heat meant he was desperately thirsty. It was part of the agony of crucifixion. Jesus' cry, however, was no polite request for a glass of water. It was a cry yearning for someone or something to ease the burning pain. Anyone who has experienced any of the side effects of dehydration will appreciate something of what Jesus was going through. Nevertheless, Jesus was not delirious.

John gives an insight into Jesus' frame of mind. He tells us that Jesus knew all was now completed. He had an awareness of God's greater plan in the midst of his pain. He understood that the end of his sufferings on our behalf was at hand. As one writer said, Jesus was still clear-minded and his memory unaffected.[227] The task that God had given him to do was nearly completed and the final part, his death, was now imminent.

It is not immediately apparent what scripture was fulfilled when Jesus said, 'I am thirsty', although it seems likely that he was referring to one of the psalms.[228] While Jesus was fulfilling prophecy, there were a number of things of profound significance behind his fifth cry from the cross.

---

226. Mark 15:25, 34.
227. Marcus Loane, *The Voice of the Cross*, p.73.
228. Psalm 69:21 and Psalm 22:15 are both possibilities.

His humanity

The phrase *I am thirsty* is just one word in the original Greek. This is the only one of the seven cries which conveys something of the physical suffering Jesus experienced. Philip Greenslade makes the point that Jesus' three years of ministry began with a period of prolonged hunger and ended on the cross in extreme thirst.[229] Jesus clearly knew what it was to be hungry and thirsty. Yet God doesn't thirst. Angelic beings don't thirst. Christians who have died and are now in heaven don't thirst.[230] But we do. Jesus' thirst, while he was dying in our place, showed his complete identification with all of humanity. The Letter to the Hebrews tells us that he shared our humanity.[231] He was just like us in every way except one. Crucially, he never sinned.

It was C. H. Spurgeon who once said:

> *Who was this that said, 'I thirst'? It was he who balanced the clouds and filled the channels of the mighty deep . . . Yes he who guided every river in its course and watered all the fields with grateful showers – he it was, the King of Kings and Lord of Lords, before whom hell trembles and the earth is filled with dismay, he whom heaven adores and all eternity worships – he it was who said, 'I thirst'! Matchless condescension – from the infinity of God to the weakness of a thirsting dying man! And this was for you.*[232]

---

229. Philip Greenslade, *Voice from the Hills*, p.167.
230. Revelation 7:16.
231. Hebrews 2:14.
232. *Spurgeon's Sermons*, Thursday 18 December 1913.

'The Well'

This is not the first time John tells us that Jesus had been thirsty. In John's Gospel we read of him tired and resting at a well near Sychar. While waiting for his disciples, he met a woman getting water and asked her to give him a drink. Even though he was thirsty, he used the moment as an opportunity to strike up a conversation with her. As they talked, he told her about the living water that only he could give her. He said, 'Whoever drinks the water I give him will never thirst. Indeed the water I give him will become in him a spring of water welling up to eternal life.'[233] Interestingly, we are not told whether the woman actually gave him a drink although she clearly had a drink of the living water that Jesus offered her! Following this conversation, she became one of his followers.[234]

It is impossible to hear Jesus' cry on the cross without thinking of this encounter with the woman at the well. Jesus was pointing us to the living God. Physical thirst can be quenched by the provision of water but it is far more important that our spiritual thirst is satisfied by 'living water' from God himself. Anyone who drinks this 'water' will never thirst again. All of us have moments when life doesn't work out as planned, times when we struggle with hurt, disappointment and grief. Equally, we know that when things are going well it won't last forever. Life itself is, at best, brief, here today but gone tomorrow. Jesus' words on the cross give us sure and certain hope. He knows what it is to experience life as a man, and because of this he knows how to help us find true and lasting fulfilment. In The Message version of the Bible we are told that Jesus came 'for people like us . . . That's why he had to enter

---

233. John 4:14.
234. John 4:29.

into every detail of human life. Then, when he came before God as high priest to get rid of the people's sins, he would have already experienced it all himself – all the pain, all the testing – and would be able to help where help was needed.'[235]

His longing

Behind this cry was his longing for the presence of his Father. 'I am thirsty' echoes the emotions expressed by the psalmist who said his soul longed for God's presence like a deer pants for water.[236] More poignantly, we are reminded of where the psalmist says, 'O God, you are my God, earnestly I seek you; my soul thirsts for you, my body longs for you, in a dry and weary land where there is no water.'[237] We cannot help but be struck by Jesus' unquenchable desire to do his Father's will despite the physical pain. Already while on the cross, Jesus had refused wine mixed with gall or myrrh,[238] which was a natural sedative. He wasn't going to allow anything to prevent himself from consciously bearing the full weight and cost of our sin.

No one before Jesus had trusted God completely. All were flawed human beings tainted by Adam's inherited sin. Jesus was different. In his darkest moment he didn't give in to frustration like Moses. He didn't lash out at those who had done this to him and who had no idea what they were doing. Instead, Jesus longed for God's presence. This was the only thing that could carry him through his hour of testing. Only God could meet his deepest need. It is no wonder that he cried out 'I am thirsty'

---

235. Hebrews 2:17, 18 [The Message].
236. Psalm 42:1, 2.
237. Psalm 63:1.
238. Matthew 27:34; Mark 15:23.

just after he had uttered the awful cry 'My God, my God, why have you forsaken me?' At the moment when others turn back from trusting God, Jesus pressed through. We will be grateful for all eternity that he did.

His offer

Only John records this cry. It should come as no surprise then that the explanation for it is hidden in his Gospel. Before this cry from the cross John recorded five other references made by Jesus to thirst or being thirsty. We have already considered three in the passage with the woman at the well.[239] On another occasion, Jesus talked to a crowd and declared that those who believed in him would never thirst.[240] Finally, John tells us that he preached at the Temple on this theme. He stood up (teachers usually sat down to teach) and loudly proclaimed that if people were thirsty they needed to come to him to have their thirst quenched.[241] In saying this, Jesus was picking up God's great promise from the Old Testament that he would quench the thirst of desperate souls at no cost.[242]

Whilst we know only God can satisfy our thirst,[243] the truth is that we all try to quench our spiritual thirst without him. Many years ago someone I knew rang me, desperate for help. He owed money to a drug dealer who was threatening him. This person was a Christian but still had a long-standing, life-controlling addiction. I probably made a bad decision on the spur of the moment. I agreed to lend him the money to

---

239. John 4:13-15.
240. John 6:35.
241. John 7:37, 38.
242. Isaiah 55:1.
243. Psalm 107:9.

pay off the debt. We drove to an empty car park and I gave him the necessary cash. I stayed in the car because he thought the dealer might be 'spooked' by the possibility that I was an undercover police officer. As he walked away from the car, I contemplated my mistake. I had no idea whether he was going to pay the dealer, pocket the money or buy more drugs. In the moment, I also realised that I was being recorded on the car park's security camera. I had visions of being on Crimewatch: 'Does anyone recognise this car or this man?' Fortunately for me, nothing further came of it as the dealer was happy with the outcome and I did not end up on prime time television! I wish I could say everything changed for my friend from that moment forward. Unfortunately not. The addiction continued. Yet in the end he became so 'thirsty' for help that he eventually threw himself completely on Christ, the source of 'living water'. He came to understand all that Jesus had done for him on the cross and what that now meant for him as a follower of Jesus. He found freedom in Christ. It wasn't the end of his battles but, as C. S. Lewis observed of Edmund in *The Voyage of the Dawn Treader*, the cure had started.

All our addictions, all the things that we put before God, are false ways of quenching the deep thirst in our hearts. A love of money, the need to control, depending even on good things such as family, education and relationships to give us meaning, can prevent us from relying on God to ultimately satisfy us. None of these other things will fully meet our deepest needs. Ecclesiastes enigmatically reminds us: 'All streams flow into the sea, yet the sea is never full.'[244] When we try to fill the void in our hearts by any other means we turn our back on God, the

---

244. Ecclesiastes 1:7.

spring of living water.[245] We attempt to satisfy our thirst with things that will only ever give temporary respite. How many of us have fallen into this trap?

Jesus' desire to do his Father's will put him on the cross. He – the source of living water – became thirsty so that we need never be thirsty again.[246] Paul tells the church in Corinth that the children of Israel in the desert 'drank from the spiritual rock that accompanied them, and that rock was Christ'.[247] You will remember Moses made the mistake of striking the rock to get life-giving water. God had told him all he had to do was speak to it. We must learn to avoid doing the same as Moses. None of us needs to 'strike the rock' any more because Jesus was struck once for all on the cross. All we need do is speak to the rock. We simply come to him and ask. As Jesus himself said to the woman at the well, 'If you knew the gift of God and who it is that asks you for a drink, you would have asked him and he would have given you living water.'[248] Too often we try to justify ourselves and earn God's favour. When will we learn we cannot 'buy' God's free gift? When we slip into legalism and step out of grace, we start to strike the rock. Our efforts will get us nowhere. It is not about what we do, it is about what he has already done. All we need do is ask and rest in the finished work of Christ.

The world around us is full of broken and needy people. All of them are thirsty. All of them need the living water that Christ offers. The cross brings us to the only place where we can drink freely and without cost. On the wall in Mother Teresa's

---
245. Jeremiah 2:13; 17:13.
246. 2 Corinthians 8:9.
247. 1 Corinthians 10:4.
248. John 4:10.

Missionaries of Charity chapels is a crucifix with the following words: 'I thirst.' The charity aims to quench Jesus' thirst as they meet the needs of the poor and broken. Mother Teresa herself found Jesus was the living water that truly satisfied. From then on she sought to bring every needy soul she met to Christ. In meeting their needs she believed she was acknowledging the thirst of Jesus on the cross for the souls of others.

In Matthew's Gospel, Jesus is recorded telling a parable of sheep and goats. He commends some, the sheep, because they gave him something to drink when he was thirsty. Jesus is saying that he associates himself so much with his followers that when they are thirsty so is he! As we meet the needs of the poor and needy out of the living water we have ourselves received, we are doing it personally for Jesus. He promises that there is a day coming when there will be no more thirsty people.[249]

Are we thirsty?

What should our response be to this cry from the cross? The Roman soldiers' response was seemingly one of sympathy. They gave him some of their cheap sour wine on a sponge. The crowd mocked him. Most of the people in Jerusalem that day were just indifferent. Can I suggest our response should be to cry out to the only one who can truly satisfy? All through the Bible, God hears the cry of the thirsty. Whether we are an abandoned mother like Hagar[250] or a burned-out leader like Elijah, ending up in a dry and barren place,[251] there is hope for us.

---

249. Revelation 21:6; 22:17.
250. Genesis 21:14-19.
251. 1 Kings 19:3-8.

As we put our trust in Christ through worship, prayer, reading (and applying) what God has said in the Bible, and fellowship with other believers, he renews our strength. In doing so, he quenches our thirst with the living water that he freely gives and we are able to get up and go again.[252]

I want to finish with what C. S. Lewis writes in *The Silver Chair*. Jill is thirsty and comes to the lion, Aslan, whom Lewis uses as an analogy for Christ. She has to pass by Aslan in order to quench her desperate thirst in the stream but she is afraid. In order to drink she has to trust him.

> *'Are you not thirsty?' said the lion. 'I'm dying of thirst,' said Jill. 'Then drink,' said the lion. 'May I – could I – would you mind going away while I do?' said Jill. The lion answered this only by a look and very low growl. As Jill gazed at its motionless bulk, she realised that she might as well have asked the whole mountain to move aside for her convenience. The delicious rippling noise of the stream was driving her nearly frantic. 'Will you promise not to – do anything to me, if I do come?' said Jill. 'I make no such promise,' said the lion. Jill was so thirsty now that, without noticing it, she had come a step nearer the lion . . . 'I daren't come and drink,' said Jill. 'Then you will die of thirst,' said the lion. 'Oh dear!' said Jill, coming another step nearer. 'I suppose I must go and look for another stream then.' The lion said, 'There is no other stream.'*

---

252. Isaiah 40:31.

There is only one place to find living water that will truly satisfy the soul. The question is – will we come and drink? Jesus' invitation still stands: 'If anyone is thirsty, let him come to me and drink.'[253]

---

253. John 7:37.

CHAPTER 7

MISSION ACCOMPLISHED

'Mission Accomplished'

> *When he had received the drink, Jesus said, 'It is finished.' With that, he bowed his head and gave up his spirit.*
>
> (John 19:30)

'Houston, we have a problem.' This familiar but fictitious quote was made most famous in the Oscar winning film *Apollo 13*. The movie was based on the actual events surrounding the 1970 Apollo 13 space mission. After several days in space, an oxygen tank exploded, causing serious damage to the command module. The planned moon landing had to be abandoned. NASA had to quickly devise a way to get the three astronauts back home. Ingeniously, they used the gravitational pull of the moon to 'slingshot' the lunar module back towards earth. NASA also managed to resolve, amongst other things, the astronauts' critical need of water, increasing their chances of surviving the return journey. On re-entry, everyone at Mission Control was on tenterhooks as the communication silence was longer than predicted – by some 90 seconds. This may not sound a lot but at the time it felt like an eternity. Eventually, in the most difficult of circumstances, the crew of Apollo 13 made it home unharmed. Mission accomplished.

It wasn't Jesus who had a problem. It was us. We were separated from God and needed saving. Jesus was on his way to rescue us. At the cross, when it looked like it had all gone wrong, God was still in complete control. Jesus' mission was about to be accomplished. He was going home. It is at this point that we hear Jesus' sixth cry which is only recorded for us in John's Gospel. Previous cries from the cross have shown Jesus thirsty and out of contact with his Father. As we reach the final moments of his mission, the communication silence is over and his thirst for his Father's presence has been quenched. Jesus says, 'It is finished.' It is these three simple words that we are going to unpack.

When I have been on one of my do-it-yourself adventures and finally reached the end, there are two shouts that resound through the house. Annie's cry is understandably: 'Thank goodness that's over.' Mine is, 'I've done it!' . . . Well, sometimes anyway. It would be easy for us to conclude that Jesus was just saying 'it's over' or 'I'm finished.' If we did, we'd be wrong, because that isn't what he meant at all. John uses the same word elsewhere in his Gospel and it always means 'it is completed or perfected'. Only one word is used in Greek: 'tetelestai'. John uses the word in its future tense, meaning it is a past act with a present effect. He is making it clear that it is finished and it will forever stay finished.[254]

History is littered with projects that have never been finished. Charles Dickens' last book, *The Mystery of Edwin Drood*, was one of them. The main character, Edwin Drood, has disappeared. It was suspected that he had been murdered. Unfortunately, the mystery was never going to be resolved as Dickens died halfway through writing the book. Even though he was about to die, Jesus was declaring he had completed everything his Father had sent him to do. 'It is finished' are the most thrilling words we will ever hear.

Yet what had been accomplished? What was finished? Whilst we may never fully plumb the depths of this phrase[255] on this side of eternity, the Bible does give us some indication of what Jesus meant.

---

254. John Stott, The Cross of Christ, p.82.
255. For an article on how 'tetelestai' was allegedly used in early Greek culture, see http://www.preceptaustin.org/tetelestai-paid_in_full.

Suffering ceased

Kurt Cobain found fame in the 1990s as the lead singer of the band, Nirvana. He once said: 'Nirvana means freedom from pain, suffering and the external world, and that's pretty close to my definition of punk rock.'

Tragically, at 27 years old, he committed suicide. Sadly, suffering in this world cannot be avoided. We see it on a global scale in earthquakes, famines and floods. We see it in community tragedies when planes crash, buildings collapse, boats sink and people are massacred. We see it at an individual level in the lives of people affected by bereavement, sickness, handicap, divorce, broken relationships, depression, loneliness, involuntary singleness, redundancy . . . The list goes on and on. Suffering touches all of our lives. Yet no one ever suffered like Jesus.

Jesus, whilst being completely God, experienced life just like us.[256] He spent the three years prior to this moment bringing people relief from suffering. Even though he regularly healed the sick[257] he never promised the people he healed that they wouldn't suffer in this world again. People whom he loved died. He saw, at first hand, the anguish and pain that suffering caused. He himself was scourged and brutally beaten[258] before he underwent the horror of a Roman crucifixion. He experienced the emotional and mental torment of knowing what he was going to suffer before any sentence had been passed.[259] Yet far worse than all of this, on the cross he faced the anger of a just and holy God for our wrongdoing.[260] He

---
256. Romans 1:3, 4; Hebrews 2:14.
257. Matthew 8:16.
258. John 19:1-3.
259. Luke 22:41-44.
260. Romans 5:9.

wouldn't have been human if he wasn't glad that all of this was about to come to an end.

Yet Jesus' cry was not one of relief but of victory. This is good news for all of us. We are all guaranteed to experience suffering. Jesus' cry tells us that his suffering ended and it holds out a promise that one day ours will too. All who put their faith in him in this life will be with him forever. In the next life we are told there will be no more pain or tears.[261] As the American author Charles Swindoll makes clear, God is the expert who can restore our soul when our suffering seems unbearable. Yet it is only through our faith in Jesus that we will ever experience his peace.[262]

Prophecy fulfilled

There are lots of things I would never do if I knew all the facts. Annie says my problem, if I remember correctly, is that most of the time I don't pay attention! This is not an issue with God. He never regrets doing something because he didn't know all the facts. He is never surprised or caught out. There is a simple but profound reason. God is. You will remember God told Moses that his name was, 'I am who I am.'[263] God exists outside of space and time. More accurately, space and time only exist in him. This means he knows everything. The evidence of this runs right through the Bible. God lets us 'in' on some of what is going to happen – we call these prophecies.

The focus of many of these prophecies in the Old Testament is the Messiah, God's promised deliverer. Isaiah told us that he would be a suffering servant.[264] Daniel said he would be like

---

261. Revelation 21:4.
262. Charles Swindoll, *Growing Strong in the Seasons of Life* (Zondervan, 1994), p.166.
263. Exodus 3:14.
264. Isaiah 52:13–53:12.

a son of man.[265] Zechariah described him as a king bringing salvation.[266] It is also clear that Jesus' death on a Roman cross was part of God's great plan.[267] We have already seen prophecy after prophecy accurately foretelling what would happen to Jesus on the cross. There are several occasions when the Gospel writers tell us that Jesus knew that everything was now fulfilled.[268]

All the hints in the Old Testament about a coming Messiah are satisfied by Jesus. All the New Testament prophecies are and will be fulfilled in him. Jesus completed what God sent him to do.[269] In response to Jesus' cry, 'It is finished', we need to fix our eyes on Jesus, the author and perfecter of our faith.[270] It is only through him that we can enjoy a relationship with the living God.

Satan defeated

One of the main battlegrounds of World War II was in North Africa. A key moment in the Allies' eventual victory was when Montgomery defeated Rommel at El Alamein. Rommel, 'the Desert Fox', was a formidable opponent. Apparently, Montgomery had a picture of Rommel hanging in his command tent where he could see it every day. He never wanted to forget who he was fighting. We must do the same. As we read through the Bible we become increasingly aware that there is an enemy opposed to God. There are moments when we see him exposed but mostly he is hidden from view. In the Garden of Eden we

---

265. Daniel 7:13, 14.
266. Zechariah 9:9.
267. Acts 2:23.
268. John 19:28.
269. John 4:34; 5:36; 17:4.
270. Hebrews 12:2.

see how the devil first deceived Adam. As a result, death, which is fundamentally separation from God, became our new reality.[271] Yet even at the lowest moment, when all seemed lost, God promised that a day would come when 'the seed' of Adam would crush the devil.[272] At the cross, that day finally arrived.[273]

The devil is a murderer, a liar and a thief.[274] Death is his calling card. He wants nothing more than for men and women to be eternally separated from God their Creator. John tells us that the reason Jesus came was to destroy the devil's work.[275] The writer of Hebrews makes it clear that, 'Since the children have flesh and blood, he too shared in their humanity so that by his death he might destroy him who holds the power of death – that is, the devil – and free those who all their lives were held in slavery by their fear of death.'[276]

In Roman times, when a prisoner was convicted, the charge against him was written on a sheet. It was either attached to the door of the cell or, as we have seen in Jesus' case, nailed to the cross. Jesus' charge was 'This is the King of the Jews.' Some charge! Once the prisoner had served his sentence, presuming it was not a capital crime, he was released. Apparently, 'tetelestai' was written across the charge sheet. It was then his to keep, so all would know his sentence had been served. Jesus, the seed of Adam, proclaimed 'It is finished' because through his death he had restored all that Adam had lost.[277] The sting of death had been pulled. The devil's calling card had been trumped.

---

271. Romans 5:12.
272. Genesis 3:15.
273. Hebrews 2:14.
274. John 8:44.
275. 1 John 3:8.
276. Hebrews 2:14, 15.
277. Romans 5:17.

Sin atoned for

'Tetelestai' was an everyday Greek word used in the first century.[278] As such, it would have been used in a number of contexts. One place where it seems it would have been regularly heard was in the Temple courts in Jerusalem. The priests, who were responsible for what went on inside the Temple, had a number of tasks. One was to ensure that the animals being offered as sacrifices were acceptable. Each one had to be blemish-free. God would not accept animals that were not perfect.[279] Once the animal was checked over and found to be acceptable, the priest said 'tetelestai'. It is done. The sacrifice was acceptable.

The sins of the people were then transferred to the animal by the priest before it was killed. It died as a substitute for the people. The punishment for sin is always the same – death.[280] As we have seen, the Apostle John refers to Jesus as the Lamb of God who takes away the sin of the world.[281] Jesus came to be our substitute. He was spotless and blameless. Everyone recognised that this was true, including Pilate, the Roman centurion looking on and even one of the two criminals being executed alongside Jesus. Yet it was God's assessment that counted and he accepted Jesus' death in our stead. The Bible says that not only was Jesus our spotless lamb but he was also our great High Priest.[282] This is why it was Jesus who cried out: 'tetelestai'. The New Testament writers tell us that 'we have been made holy through the sacrifice of the body of Jesus Christ once for all'.[283]

---

278. See footnote 255.
279. Malachi 1:8.
280. Romans 6:23.
281. John 1:29.
282. Hebrews 4:14, 15.
283. Hebrews 10:10.

Jesus' blood has been shed for us. It cleanses us completely. 'It is finished' is all we need to hear. When we struggle to believe that this is true, we are like prisoners trapped inside a locked prison cell. The key, however, is on the inside. We simply need to believe the truth and the truth will set us free.[284] There was a time when I never thought God would forgive me. Actually, the problem wasn't God, it was me. I was deeply ashamed of things I'd done. I was wracked with guilt. My Christian life was schizophrenic. In public I put on a mask but away from people I was broken. Then, one day, God engineered that I meet with someone who openly talked about things that were issues to me. As he talked all I could think was, 'I hope no one is listening; if they are, they will guess my secret.' Then the penny dropped. The person I was talking to was free and I wasn't. I still remember him explaining to me what the writer of Hebrews said. If Jesus, the unblemished Son of God, offered himself in our place before God, how much more will his blood cleanse our consciences from acts that lead to death, so that we can serve the living God.[285] My sin was paid for at the cross once and for all.

Law satisfied

I'm sad to say I've broken the law. Sometimes wilfully, sometimes accidentally. Sometimes I didn't even know I'd broken it. It didn't matter anyway. The law is the law. And as far as God is concerned, his law is good.[286] Sadly for us, it sets an impossible benchmark. We can only draw near to a holy God if our hearts

---
284. John 8:32.
285. Hebrews 9:14.
286. Romans 7:7-13.

are pure and our hands are clean.[287] Unfortunately, we all fall short, whether by a metre or a mile.[288] The problem is in us.[289] I well remember the years, in my late teens and early twenties, that I played religious 'snakes and ladders'. It involved me going to church services knowing that I'd let God down. I would ask for forgiveness and then make promises I couldn't keep, or had no intention of keeping. I'd leave the building feeling I had made progress, only to find that by the following Sunday I was back at square one. It was hopeless. Actually, I was hopeless. God couldn't lower the bar.[290] I needed help, which was exactly the point of God's law.[291] It was always intended to lead us to Jesus. God sent his Son to solve our problem. As a man, he never fell short of God's standard.[292] Sin had separated us from God but Jesus fulfilled the requirements of the law on our behalf forever. He is the only acceptable sacrifice for our sin.[293]

When Jesus cried out 'It is finished', he was declaring before the courts of heaven that the law had been satisfied. If we have put our trust in him then he has fulfilled the law on our behalf.[294] Thereafter, God's Spirit enables us to live for God.[295]

I have a good friend who, during a Sunday morning gathering at our church, had a revelation that God was no longer angry with him. He finally understood the truth. Other people may still have been angry with him but God wasn't! For years, in his own head, he'd mistakenly lived under a cloud. Jesus has satisfied the law. God is not angry with us. It is finished.

---

287. Psalm 24:3, 4.
288. Romans 3:23.
289. Romans 8:3.
290. Matthew 5:17, 18; Luke 16:17.
291. Galatians 3:24.
292. Hebrews 2:10.
293. 1 John 2:2; 4:10.
294. Romans 10:4.
295. Galatians 5:18.

Redemption secured

In Jesus' day, merchants used the word 'tetelestai' as part of their business transactions. It meant that the debt was paid in full. It had important legal connotations. In a Roman slave market, when a slave was purchased, 'tetelestai' was written across the document of purchase. The slave was no longer the property of the previous owner. This undergirds the biblical term 'redeemed'. It is the gaining (or regaining) possession of something in exchange for payment, or the clearing of a debt. As we all inherited Adam's sin,[296] we came under the control of the devil and his kingdom of darkness. When we come to faith in Christ, the Bible says we are redeemed.[297] We are bought at a price[298] and brought out of darkness into God's marvellous light.[299]

Jesus has secured eternal redemption for us.[300] Mark tells us that Jesus came 'to give his life as a ransom for many'.[301] Paul puts it in his own inimitable style: 'In him we have redemption through his blood, the forgiveness of sins, in accordance with the riches of God's grace that he lavished on us with all wisdom and understanding.'[302] When he appeared utterly defeated on the cross, Jesus proclaimed his victory. His was a cry of triumph. It still sounds today over all our difficulties, problems and situations. Let me explain . . .

As an avid football fan I support Southampton FC. Over the years 'The Saints' have battled against relegation many times.

---

296. Romans 5:12.
297. Galatians 3:13.
298. 1 Corinthians 6:20.
299. 1 Peter 2:9.
300. Hebrews 9:12.
301. Mark 10:45.
302. Ephesians 1:7, 8.

There have been moments at the end of the season when we have been losing in a key game. Relegation is looking like a serious probability. Suddenly, during the game, the crowd at St Mary's Stadium start to cheer. They rise to their feet and begin to sing, even though it looks like we are going to be defeated. Why? A victory has been won elsewhere that has saved us. Each one of us can be facing failure and defeat and yet we too can rejoice because of the victory of Christ.[303]

Relationship restored

In the Old National Gallery in Berlin there is a painting by Adolph Menzel. He intended to paint Frederick the Great speaking with some of his generals before a key battle. Menzel started by painting the generals and the surroundings in all their glory. Next he drew an outline of Frederick in charcoal. Then, unfortunately, he died. The unfinished painting still hangs in the gallery. In the Garden of Eden, God's masterpiece was ruined by Adam's 'death', his separation from God. God was no longer at the centre of the people he had created. Ever after, God planned to restore his masterpiece. He sent Jesus to complete the work.

Humanity had no idea what God was like. We had a sketch in our heads but it was all a bit monochromatic, black and white. We knew God was great but we had no idea that he was loving. Jesus started to repaint the picture of what God was like.[304] Philip asked him to show the disciples his Father. Jesus said that anyone who had seen him had seen

---
303. James 1:2-4.
304. John 17:6.

the Father.[305] Jesus' primary aim was to bring us back into relationship with 'Abba',[306] the intimate name for his Father. Jesus came to restore what Adam's sin had ruined.

Jesus' death on the cross shows us the Father's heart. The love of God is laid bare for all. He so loved us he sent his precious Son to die for us. Anyone who believes in Jesus will be with him forever.[307] Jesus has enabled us to be restored into relationship with God the Father.[308] The Bible calls this reconciliation. Paul urged the Corinthian believers and us to '[b]e reconciled to God. God made him who had no sin to be sin for us, so that in him we might become the righteousness of God.'[309]

Apparently, when an artist had put the final brushstroke on his painting he would say, 'tetelestai'. It is now complete. Jesus' cry tells us that God's masterpiece has been restored to its intended glory. God, in all his glory, is back in his rightful place at the centre of his people. We can know him as our Father through Jesus Christ. It is finished indeed!

Job done

Finally, it is said that 'tetelestai' was also a phrase used by servants who had completed a task for their master. If so, there is no better word to sum up what unfolded on the cross on that first Good Friday. Jesus completed the work that God had given him to do. This really is good news. If we are fearful . . . suffering . . . struggling with doubts . . . wracked with guilt . . .

---

305. John 14:9.
306. Romans 8:15.
307. John 3:16.
308. 2 Corinthians 5:18.
309. 2 Corinthians 5:20, 21.

feeling distant from God . . . then there is no better antidote than to remind ourselves of what Jesus accomplished on the cross for us.

J. C. Ryle put it like this: 'It is surely not too much to say, that of all the seven famous sayings of Christ on the cross, none is more remarkable than "tetelestai".' He goes on to say: 'We need not fear that either sin or Satan or law shall condemn us at the last day. We may lean back on the thought, that we have a Saviour who has done all, paid all, accomplished all, performed all that is necessary for our salvation.'[310] 'Tetelestai' declares that when we stand before the judgement seat of God none of us will be found wanting.[311]

Mission accomplished.

'The writing is on the Wall – weighed but not wanting'

---

310. J. C. Ryle, *Expository Thoughts on the Gospels: John*, Vol.3, p.355.
311. Daniel 5:27.

CHAPTER 8

THE HANDS OF GOD

'We Shall Go No Lower'

> *It was now about the sixth hour, and darkness came over the whole land until the ninth hour, for the sun stopped shining. And the curtain of the temple was torn in two. Jesus called out with a loud voice, 'Father, into your hands I commit my spirit.' When he had said this, he breathed his last. The centurion, seeing what had happened, praised God and said, 'Surely this was a righteous man.' When all the people who had gathered to witness this sight saw what took place, they beat their breasts and went away. But all those who knew him, including the women who had followed him from Galilee, stood at a distance, watching these things.*
>
> (Luke 23:44-49)

In 1986 Argentina beat England 2-1 in the Quarter Finals of the World Cup. The game was notable for two stand-out goals by Diego Maradona. Football pundits still say the second goal was one of the best ever scored in the World Cup Finals. However, the first goal should not have been allowed to stand. Maradona, with some dexterity, flicked the ball past the English goalkeeper, Peter Shilton, with his hand. In the press conference after the game, bizarrely, Maradona said the contentious goal was only partly due to his head. The rest was due to the hand of God. I don't think there was anyone who thought God had a hand in the goal. He couldn't have. God doesn't have hands!

The Bible tells us that God is spirit[312] and therefore doesn't have a body. Having said that, God has chosen to reveal what he is like in a way which is easy for us to understand. The Bible

---

312. John 4:24.

uses a literary tool called anthropomorphism. Essentially, it attributes human characteristics to God when referring to him. This explains why we are told that God can speak, see and think and why we read about God's voice,[313] eyes[314] and mind.[315] In the same way the Bible often refers to the hands of God.

In the Old Testament there are numerous references to his hands. The idiom is used to convey how powerful he is[316] as well as to reveal how he helps us.[317] Isaiah tells us that God doesn't forget the names of people who love him because their names are written on his hands.[318] He also says God will take hold of our hand when we are afraid.[319] Similarly, in the New Testament, Peter encourages us to humble ourselves under God's mighty hand.[320] John reminds us that no one can take us out of our Father's hand.[321] God's hands are literally all over the Bible.

In the last of Jesus' cries from the cross, he commits his spirit into his Father's hands. As his sufferings come to an end, he turns to rest in God. This is the biblical pattern. Six days of creation, then God rested.[322] Six days of work, and then we ought to take a day off to recuperate and spend some time with God.[323] When Jesus cries out for the seventh and last time, his work on the cross is finished. Now it is time for his spirit to rest in God's hands. If we were unsure, we are about to find that there is no safer place to be.

---

313. Psalm 29:3-9.
314. 2 Chronicles 16:9.
315. Psalm 110:4.
316. Exodus 15:6.
317. Psalm 44:3.
318. Isaiah 49:16.
319. Isaiah 41:13.
320. 1 Peter 5:6.
321. John 10:29.
322. Genesis 2: 2, 3.
323. Exodus 20:8-10.

God shows his hand

The events that live longest in our memories are those marked by something unexpected happening. I will always remember when my then six-year-old son, Joe, lost his front tooth. He'd been riding his bike too fast round a bend when he lost control. Inadvertently, he used his head to stop himself. His front tooth was knocked clean out. The lamp post was unmoved. I took a day off work to look after him. In the morning we sat together and I read to him for a while. Then I switched on the television and in stunned silence we watched the collapse of the twin towers of the World Trade Centre. Neither of us will forget the events of 11 September 2001.

Pontius Pilate, the Jewish religious leaders and the Roman soldiers thought that by executing Jesus they were getting rid of a troublemaker. They wanted it all to be over quickly and then swept under the carpet. God had no intention of allowing that to happen. He ensured that no one would forget this day. Deep darkness enveloped the entire land. It was as if the hand of God had stopped the sun shining on what was happening outside Jerusalem. No wonder Marcus Loane concluded that something happened in the natural world that was so extraordinary it could only be attributed to the intervention of God.[324]

Mark tells us[325] that Jesus was nailed to the cross at roughly nine o'clock in the morning. As it was the preparation day before the Passover Sabbath, the religious leaders expected the executions to be completed within the day. Jesus had been on the cross for three hours when the light disappeared. For the next three hours darkness enveloped everything. Luke

---

324. Marcus Loane, *The Voice of the Cross*, p.60.
325. Mark 15:25.

simply says the sun stopped shining.[326] There was no natural explanation. It was not a solar eclipse because the Passover always fell at full moon. Solar eclipses can only occur when there is a new moon. Darkness engulfed what should have been the brightest part of the day. It was as if creation itself could not bear to look on what was unfolding on this bleak Judean hillside.

As we have seen, the darkness was a sign of the judgement of God on our sin which Jesus was bearing. John tells us, 'God is light, and in him is no darkness at all.'[327] God could not look on his Son who was effectively carrying our sin. The last doom of all those who have turned their back on God is darkness, which tells us that in those three hours, Jesus bore the punishment that should have been ours.

Some years later we read of Paul travelling to Cyprus. On arriving in Paphos, he was introduced to the proconsul, Sergius Paulus. He invited Paul to tell him the good news about Jesus. Unfortunately, it became complicated because the proconsul's attendant, Elymas, was endeavouring to undermine what Paul was saying. He clearly didn't want his employer to become a follower of Jesus. Eventually, Paul had had enough. He told Elymas that, because he was trying to prevent what God was doing, God's hand was against him. The consequence was that he would be blind for a season. We are told, 'Immediately . . . darkness came over him'. Having seen all of this, Sergius Paulus became a believer.[328] One cannot help but notice some similarities with what we have been considering. The 'hand of God' caused the light of the sun to be kept from Elymas. It was

---

326. Luke 23:45.
327. 1 John 1:5.
328. Acts 13:6-12.

the judgement of God on his sin, his rebellion against God. The darkness would only last for a season. Under the grace of God there was still hope for Elymas, but only if he personally put his trust in Jesus.

A gesture used to show that you are not listening to someone involves raising your hand, palm forward towards their face. Effectively, you are saying, 'Talk to the hand because the face ain't listening.' As Jesus hung on the cross, it was as if God had raised his hand.[329] Sin was being dealt with, once and for all, and God turned his face away.

God takes matters into his own hands

Not only did the sun stop shining but the Temple curtain was torn in two. This curtain separated off the holiest part of the Temple, called the Most Holy Place. Behind the curtain was kept the Ark of the Covenant which contained the law of God. This was the place where God had promised to dwell among his people.[330] The curtain was there to protect people from the awesome presence of God. No one could see God and live.[331] The only person allowed behind this curtain was the High Priest. God allowed him to enter once a year at the Passover. He carried blood from the lamb which had been sacrificed for the nation's sin into God's presence. He then sprinkled this blood on the lid of the Ark, also called the 'Mercy Seat'. God would then forgive the people for their sin. It may seem a bit gory but dealing with sin is a serious business.

---

329. Isaiah 9:12, 17, 21.
330. Exodus 25:8; 40:34, 35.
331. Exodus 33:20.

Matthew tells us that the curtain was ripped asunder, in situ, from top to bottom.[332] This was not humanly possible. The curtain was around 60 feet high, 15 feet wide and was as thick as the palm of a man's hand. No one person could have torn the curtain in two, top down. It could only be the 'hand of God'. God was declaring that, because Jesus' blood had been shed on the cross, no more sacrifices were necessary.[333] Access into his presence was no longer restricted.[334] Jesus' death on the cross was the culmination of God's plan to restore us into relationship with himself.

John Piper says, 'Over and around the death of Jesus Christ is the ruling hand of God. He has not fumbled the ball. There are no loose ends.'[335]

Jesus is in good hands

Over the years, I have watched on as friends and family have been dying. Many exuded confidence and peace because of their faith. Some seemed to know that they were about to pass into the presence of God. I have known other people who've appeared to hold on to life while completing a task or waiting to say their final goodbyes to a loved one, only to die immediately afterwards. I have never seen anything like Jesus' final moments.

My mother battled against her illness with every fibre of her being. When she was first diagnosed with cancer, I was concerned that she might refuse treatment. However, she said she would have whatever treatment the doctors recommended.

---

332. Matthew 27:51.
333. Hebrews 9:24-28.
334. Hebrews 10:19, 20.
335. 'Into Thy Hands I commit my Spirit', 20 April 1984, by John Piper. ©Desiring God Foundation. Source: desiringGod.org

Very simply, she didn't feel ready to die. She was adamant that she wouldn't give in. After four and a half years, major surgery and three courses of brutal chemotherapy, she gave up her heroic fight against cancer. By the end she was tired and weary and was ready to be with Jesus. Like many others before her, she slipped into a coma and didn't awake again this side of heaven. Jesus' end was nothing like this. He didn't pass quietly out of this world. His last words rang loudly with conviction and certainty. He may have been physically weak but his spirit was unbreakable.

'Father'

Most of what needs to be said about Jesus' relationship with God, his Father, has already been said. We have seen that his relationship with his Father was at the core of who he was. These seven cries began with Jesus calling God 'Father'.[336] We have seen the desolation when Jesus no longer knew the nearness of his Father. Now, as all is completed, he ends what he says on the cross where he started: 'Father'. Intimacy had been restored.

This is the gospel. For those who have put their personal faith in Jesus to save them this is the best news ever. Jesus has opened the way for us to experience intimacy with God: Father, Son and Holy Spirit. We can now walk in the light as he is in the light.[337] The deep darkness that enveloped us has been banished. The way into God's holy presence is now forever

---
336. Luke 23:34.
337. 1 John 1:7.

open through Jesus.[338] This is what Jesus has won for us. God loves us just as much as he loves his precious Son.[339] Amazing.

'Into your hands I commit my spirit'

In truth, for all of Jesus' life on earth, he was in his Father's hands. His continual prayer was for God's will to be done on earth as it was in heaven.[340] This is exactly what Jesus spent his life doing.[341] Yet, for a short period, Jesus chose to put himself into the hands of men. Actually, Matthew says that Jesus was 'betrayed into the hands of sinners'.[342] At one level he was betrayed. Yet if he'd wanted to, Jesus could have resisted them. No one could stand before him as the Son of God. He was, is and always will be the great 'I am'.[343] If Jesus hadn't let the mob arrest him the previous evening, there would have been nothing they could have done.[344] Now having allowed them to do their worst, Jesus commits himself back into the hands of his Father.

Jesus was quoting from the first part of a psalm of David. It said, 'Into your hands I commit my spirit; redeem me, O Lord, the God of truth.'[345] Of course Jesus didn't quote the latter half. He didn't need to cry to God to redeem him like David, because Jesus was the Redeemer! Not one of the Gospel writers say that after committing himself into his Father's hands, Jesus died. Instead, they describe him giving up his spirit. Jesus' body may have reached the end of the road but human beings are

---

338. Ephesians 3:12.
339. John 17:23-26.
340. Matthew 6:9, 10.
341. Luke 2:49.
342. Matthew 26:45; Luke 24:7.
343. John 18:5, 6.
344. Luke 4:28-30.
345. Psalm 31:5.

more than just flesh and blood. We are made up of 'spirit, soul and body'.[346] Our physical bodies die and return to the ground, 'ashes to ashes and dust to dust'. Our spirits, however, return to God,[347] who breathed life into us in the first place.[348]

No one could take Jesus' life from him. Jesus himself said, 'The reason my Father loves me is that I lay down my life ... No one takes it from me, but I lay it down of my own accord. I have authority to lay it down and authority to take it up again. This command I received from my Father.'[349] This was exactly what he did. He entrusted himself to God his Father for safekeeping.

After saying this, Jesus breathed his last. The Greek word Matthew uses literally means that Jesus dismissed his spirit.[350] The other Gospel writers say that Jesus breathed out or gave up his spirit. All of them clearly imply that Jesus *chose* the path he took. Death, 'the king of terrors',[351] held no fear for him. As far as he was concerned, death had no sting.[352] His victory on the cross had swallowed up death!

As someone once said, 'There would be no tremendous uncertain doubt or fear in his mind when the end came. He knew that in dying he would vanquish the power of death, he would open the gates of the kingdom for the people of God. The light of victory was in his eyes, the shout of victory was in his voice, as he gave his spirit into the hands of an Almighty Guardian.'[353]

---

346. 1 Thessalonians 5:23.
347. Ecclesiastes 12:7.
348. Genesis 2:7.
349. John 10:17, 18.
350. Matthew 27:50.
351. Job 18:14.
352. 1 Corinthians 15:54-57.
353. Unknown. I have been unable to find where this quote originated.

Getting it at first hand

The crowd around the cross had gathered to watch a spectacle. Earlier that day, many of them would have been part of the mob crying out for Jesus to be crucified. By the end of the show they went away beating their chests, deeply saddened. They knew there had been a terrible miscarriage of justice and, having seen what they had seen, they went home shocked. Yet they missed the key point. Jesus' death on the cross demanded a personal response. It still does.

The centurion was also moved by what he saw. He was an expert in crucifixion. This was a man who'd lived with blood on his hands. He was used to handing out rough justice. He'd seen many people crucified and watched many men die. His conclusion was telling. He had never seen anyone die like this man. He knew he'd crucified innocent people before, but his conscience had been hardened over years of enforcing so-called 'justice'. Yet as he watched from his ringside seat, something changed in his heart. What he saw was enough to convince one of the hardest of men. In the end his simple statement said it all: 'Surely this was a righteous man.' In the space of hours he went from antagonist to sceptic to believer. Mark records that the centurion said of Jesus: 'this man was the Son of God!'[354] He became convinced that Jesus was who he said he was. It seems he made a personal response. Luke says it caused him to praise God!

Many people over the centuries have found Christ to be all they need. Stephen, a leader in the early Church in Jerusalem,[355] was being stoned to death because of his faith in Jesus. The

---
354. Mark 15:39.
355. Acts 7:55, 56, 59.

Bible says that, just before he died, Stephen looked up and saw heaven opened and Jesus standing at the right hand of God. He knew faith was reality. Christ had died. Christ had risen. It caused him to be able to say with confidence, 'Lord Jesus, receive my spirit.' Many others, like John Hus and Bishops Latimer and Ridley, have said the same.

Second-hand faith doesn't work. We only get faith at first-hand by personally coming to the foot of the cross, contemplating what Jesus did for us, believing in him and worshipping God.

In safe hands

If we place our faith in what Jesus has done, death should hold no more fear for us. The Bible says that, for followers of Jesus, death is simply falling asleep.[356] We close our eyes on this life and open them in the presence of God.

Jesus' last cry fills us with confidence. He has promised that no one can pluck us out of his Father's hand. C. H. Spurgeon commented on us being safe and secure in the hands of God when he said:

> *And further, when death comes the promise shall still hold good. When we stand in the midst of Jordan, we shall be able to say with David, 'I will fear no evil, for thou art with me.' We shall descend into the grave, but we shall go no lower, for the eternal arms prevent our further fall. All through life, and at its close, we shall be upheld by the 'everlasting arms' – arms that neither flag*

---

356. John 11:11.

> *nor lose their strength, for 'the everlasting God fainteth not, neither is weary.'[357]*

Sitting on my desk is a coffee mat. I have kept it for over 25 years, since I worked in Gosport. Some believe Gosport was given the name 'God's Port' by King Stephen in 1144, after he gratefully landed there in the middle of a storm. Over time they believe the name was shortened. Whatever the truth, written on the coffee mat are the words: 'God's port, my haven.' I love the phrase. It has been true for me for the past 25 years. It will be true for the rest of my days and beyond. The words of Charles Wesley's famous hymn 'Jesu, lover of my soul' sum up what it means to be safe in the hands of God:

> Jesu, lover of my soul,
> Let me to thy bosom fly,
> While the nearer waters roll,
> While the tempest still is high.
>
> Hide me, O my Saviour, hide,
> Till the storm of life is past;
> Safe into the haven guide;
> O receive my soul at last.

---

357. C. H. Spurgeon, *Morning and Evening*, 11 November: morning reading.

'God's Port, My Harbour'

CHAPTER 9

THE SIGN OF FOUR

'The Mercy Seat'

Early on the first day of the week, while it was still dark, Mary Magdalene went to the tomb and saw that the stone had been removed from the entrance. So she came running to Simon Peter and the other disciple, the one Jesus loved, and said, 'They have taken the Lord out of the tomb, and we don't know where they have put him!' So Peter and the other disciple started for the tomb. Both were running, but the other disciple outran Peter and reached the tomb first. He bent over and looked in at the strips of linen lying there but did not go in. Then Simon Peter, who was behind him, arrived and went into the tomb. He saw the strips of linen lying there, as well as the burial cloth that had been around Jesus' head. The cloth was folded up by itself, separate from the linen. Finally the other disciple, who had reached the tomb first, also went inside. He saw and believed. (They still did not understand from Scripture that Jesus had to rise from the dead.) Then the disciples went back to their homes, but Mary stood outside the tomb crying. As she wept, she bent over to look into the tomb and saw two angels in white, seated where Jesus' body had been, one at the head and the other at the foot. They asked her, 'Woman, why are you crying?' 'They have taken my Lord away,' she said, 'and I don't know where they have put him.' At this, she turned around and saw Jesus standing there, but she did not realise that it was Jesus. He asked her, 'Woman,' he said,

"why are you crying? Who is it you are looking for?'
Thinking he was the gardener, she said, 'Sir, if you
have carried him away, tell me where you have put
him, and I will get him.' Jesus said to her, 'Mary.'
She turned toward him and cried out in Aramaic,
'Rabboni!' (which means Teacher).

(John 20:1-16)

Late one night I was woken up by unusual noises in our back garden. They weren't particularly loud but they were enough to make me get out of bed. Subtly poking my head out of the first-floor bedroom window, I witnessed a crime taking place which, as of today, is still unsolved. Teenagers were breaking into the garage and trying to steal our four bikes. Fortunately, I had caught them red-handed. As they were starting to make good their getaway, I shouted very, very loudly, 'Oi . . . what do you think you are doing?' Annie, who had been fast asleep, was startled. Our nervous next-door neighbour was terrified. The opportunist thieves ran for the hills. It was at that moment I made what was a schoolboy error. For some strange reason, which I am still unable to explain, I shouted after them, 'I know where you live!' As I said it I was thinking, 'No, I don't . . . you know where I live!' My suspicion is that this was the moment when they realised they were going to get away scot-free. In any event, all four bikes were left lying in the road. As a matter of fact, there was also a fifth bike. In their haste to make a run for it, they had left one of their own behind! Some crime! Not a case for Sherlock Holmes, I think.

Sherlock Holmes, the fictional detective created by Sir Arthur Conan Doyle, is a name synonymous with unravelling seemingly unresolvable mysteries. Part of his brilliance was in analysing the evidence and deducing what had actually happened. In one of his most famous cases, 'The Sign of Four', he was quoted as saying: 'When you have eliminated the impossible, whatever remains, however improbable, must be the truth.' What happened following the crucifixion of Jesus has taxed the minds of many people over the centuries. It would have been right up Sherlock Holmes' street.

As far as Christianity is concerned, everything hangs on Jesus' resurrection from the dead. Over the last seven chapters we have explored all that Jesus said on the cross. Far from being the confused ramblings of a deluded dying man, we have found them to be the greatest words ever spoken. They fill our hearts with hope that, beyond death's door, heaven's gates are opened to us. Yet if Jesus died and is still dead, what hope is there? The New Testament's claim that Jesus Christ is now alive is the surety of all that we hope for. As we look briefly at the evidence for the resurrection, we will find that it really is the proof of victory.

The game is afoot

No serious historian has disputed the fact that Jesus lived and was subsequently crucified. The evidence from extra-biblical sources alone, such as the Roman historian Tacitus in his work *Annals*, is conclusive. It is accepted that Jesus was beaten and then nailed to a cross for around six hours. Hanging on a cross his body would have been weakened by the loss of blood and trauma. His death was public and certified. I have said it already, but the Roman guards responsible for the executions that day were professionals. They had watched many men die. Their judgement should not be treated lightly. For them to get it wrong would have been a serious mistake; hence they were brutally efficient. The two criminals alongside Jesus were still alive and so they broke their legs. It sped up the time it took for them to die. Unexpectedly, Jesus was already dead. However, just to make sure, one of the soldiers thrust a spear into his side. The spear point punctured the pericardium, the sac surrounding the heart. John records that blood and water flowed out of the wound. The blood had separated. Today, this would be accepted as medical evidence of death. No one suggested otherwise. Subsequently, Jesus' body was taken down from the cross.[358] Later on the Friday evening it was placed in an unused tomb belonging to Joseph of Arimathaea, with Pilates' permission.[359] Then something extraordinary happened.

The Apostle Paul, quoting an early Christian creed, simply says Jesus died but then rose again from the dead three days later.[360] This was and still is the rallying cry of genuine Christianity. Without Jesus' resurrection, all that he did on the cross would be meaningless.[361] The truth of all that Jesus said and did was proved by his resurrection from the dead. Others, better able than I, have studied this in great depth and concluded that the evidence for the resurrection of Jesus would stand up in a court of law today. I want to simply draw to your attention 'four signs' which even Sherlock Holmes would have concluded supported the claims of Jesus' resurrection. The game is afoot.

---

358. John 19:34, 35.
359. Mark 15:42-47.
360. 1 Corinthians 15:4. Three days meant parts of days, not whole days.
361. 1 Corinthians 15:14.

The stone was moved

Joseph and Nicodemus, both members of the Jewish Ruling Council and both now followers of Jesus, placed Jesus' body in Joseph's tomb. This was never disputed by the religious leaders of the day. A typical tomb comprised a rock chamber with 'shelves' cut into the sides where the bodies were laid. The low entrance was closed with a large disc-like rock. It was rolled down a groove in front of the tomb until it covered the entrance. It was easily rolled into place but would have needed several people to move it in order to re-open the tomb. The tomb would have been virtually impossible to open from the inside. We are told that, early on the Sunday morning, Mary Magdalene and two others[362] went to anoint Jesus' body. Mark tells us they were unsure how they would move what he describes as a very large stone.[363] They were shocked to find that the tomb was open.

Maybe they went to the wrong tomb? I've 'lost' my car several times in big car parks so maybe it was a genuine mistake. In reality they'd seen the tomb on the Friday evening[364] and it wasn't as if there were hundreds of them! If it was the case of a simple mistake it would have been pointed out very quickly once people started saying the tomb was empty and Jesus was alive. No one did this because the location of the tomb was common knowledge, so much so that Peter alluded to the evidence of the tomb when he preached to thousands on the day of Pentecost[365] only a few weeks later. So who moved the stone? Various alternatives have been put forward: the Roman soldiers under Pilate's

---
362. Mark 16:1, 2.
363. Mark 16:3, 4.
364. Luke 23:55.
365. Acts 2:32.

instructions, the Jewish religious leaders, Joseph of Arimathea with some help, the disciples themselves or some unknown others. We will come back to this in a moment.

The missing body

When Mary looked inside the open tomb she found that Jesus' body had disappeared. Peter and John ran to the tomb and corroborated what she said. Jesus' body had gone. Can we believe the Gospel stories? There are clearly a number of discrepancies between the various accounts. Irrespective of any differences, they all agree on the fundamental fact that the tomb was empty. In this respect the discrepancies are all secondary. The apologist William Lane Craig, in addressing this issue, points out that there are two incompatible accounts of Hannibal crossing the Alps to attack Rome, and yet no one doubts that it happened.[366] Likewise no one should doubt that Jesus' body was missing.

The religious leaders or Roman authorities evidently had nothing to do with the entrance-stone being moved and the missing body. If they had they would have produced the body as soon as Jesus' disciples started saying he was alive. There is no obvious reason why Joseph would come back and move the body. It is equally unlikely that any of Jesus' disciples went to the tomb and removed the body. If they did then it would be the conspiracy to end all conspiracies, as many of them died painful deaths for proclaiming that he was alive! Notwithstanding all of this, the Gospel accounts agree on two things. First of all, Pilate gave permission for guards to be placed at the tomb.[367]

---

366. Lee Strobel, *The Case for Christ* (Zondervan, 2016), p.216.
367. Matthew 27:62-66.

Secondly, the guards, appointed by the priests, kept watch during the night prior to Mary arriving at the tomb. They even put a seal on the stone. The Jewish authorities never said there were no guards; rather, they argued that they fell asleep.[368] No one doubted that the tomb was empty. No body was ever produced, simply because there was no body to produce!

The folded grave cloths

Both Peter and John went into the tomb but we're told John believed something! Peter looked around and left unsure about what had happened. John saw the same things yet came to a clear conclusion. What did they see? In the original Greek text, it is implied that they saw the burial cloths in situ. These were exactly as they were when they had been wrapped round Jesus' body. Nearby they saw the cloth that had been over Jesus' head, folded up by itself. The aloes and myrrh placed within the grave cloths wrapped around the body by Joseph and Nicodemus were still in place. G. Campbell Morgan sums up what John realised: 'The grave cloths had not been disturbed. They were just as Joseph of Arimathaea and Nicodemus had left them. The wrappings were still there; the spices had not escaped. Moreover, the cloth, wrapped in a peculiar way about the head, was undisturbed, "folded up." That word does not mean smoothed out. The napkin was still in the folds that had been wound round the head.'[369]

Even if Jesus did not die and somehow revived in the cool of the tomb, his body was wrapped tightly in cloths made heavier by the burial spices. John's Gospel tells us Joseph used about

---

368. Matthew 28:11-15.
369. G. Campbell Morgan, *The Gospel According to John*, p.310.

75 pounds of aloes and myrrh, the equivalent of around 35 two-pound (one kilo) bags of sugar! Someone would have had to help unwind the cloths, which is exactly what happened when Lazarus was raised from the dead.[370] Anyone stealing the body would have strewn the cloths and spices around the tomb. In any event, if someone was just taking the body, why take the grave cloths off? John knew that something supernatural had happened. The grave cloths were left like a discarded chrysalis. D. A. Carson supports the view that Jesus' resurrection body passed straight through the burial clothes, including the spices. He compares it to an incident a few weeks later when Jesus appeared in a room which was locked on the inside.[371] John saw all this and he believed that Jesus had risen from the dead, even though he didn't yet appreciate that this is what had been foretold in the Old Testament.

The two angels

When Mary entered the tomb, she saw two angels clothed in white. They were seated on the ledge where Jesus' body had been laid. One was seated next to where the head of Jesus had been placed and the other was next to where his feet had been. I have often wondered whether this was significant in some way. In his book *A Heavenly Conference* the Puritan writer Richard Sibbes offers an explanation. He says this is an indication that Jesus' death and resurrection fulfilled all the Old Testament sacrifices. We have previously seen that the Ark of the Covenant was kept in the Temple. It was located in the 'Most Holy Place', behind the curtain. The High Priest could enter, once a year,

---

370. John 11:43, 44.
371. 'The Gospel According to John', *Pillar New Testament Commentary*, p.637.

to bring a sin offering for the people. The sacrifice of blood he brought was sprinkled on top of the Ark, known as the 'Mercy Seat'. On either side of the 'Mercy Seat' were two angels, cast in gold.[372] Their wings overshadowed the place of sacrifice.

Effectively, the point Sibbes was making was that Mary saw the Old Testament typology had been fulfilled by Jesus' death, even if she didn't understand it at the time. She saw two angels, one where Jesus' head had been and the other where his feet had been. In between she saw the empty grave cloths. It was as though God was declaring to all heaven and earth that every person who genuinely puts their trust in Jesus has had their sins forgiven. The body was gone and all that was left were empty cloths. The once-and-for-all sacrifice had been made. The stone was rolled away and the way into God's presence was ever open. All those who believe in Jesus could draw near.

The jury is in

All the evidence points conclusively to the fact that Jesus did indeed rise from the dead. Many people have weighed the evidence we have just briefly considered and decided it must have happened. Some have even set out with the aim of disproving Jesus' physical resurrection. Yet on weighing all the evidence, they too have concluded that it must be true and have become Christians.[373] C. S. Lewis for a long time resisted believing the gospel message, before he eventually came to a personal faith. He considered himself England's least willing convert![374]

---

372. Exodus 25:20.
373. Frank Morison, *Who Moved the Stone?* (Authentic Media, 2006); Lee Strobel, *The Case for Christ* (Zondervan, 2016).
374. C.S. Lewis, *Surprised by Joy* (Fontana, 1959), p.182.

John saw the evidence and believed. Peter initially went away thoughtful before encountering the risen Jesus personally. The Pharisees and other religious leaders simply refused to believe. The challenge today is still the same. In recent months I have spent time with several people talking through this evidence. Whilst putting our trust in what Jesus has said and done doesn't require us to throw our brain out of the window, it does require us to take a step of faith. Unbelief is fundamentally a heart issue. Voltaire apparently said, 'If a thousand people and myself saw a miracle on the streets of Paris, I would rather disbelieve two thousand eyes plus my own than believe a miracle had happened.'[375]

Mary was the first of over five hundred of Jesus' followers to see him alive.[376] Five hundred people is a remarkable number. Either they were colluding or they were telling the truth. Mass hallucinations of people all seeing the same thing simply can't happen. Many of these people were prepared to die because they were convinced Jesus had risen from the dead. They knew that what he said on the cross was true. They knew that what he accomplished on the cross was real. They were certain of where they were going. For them, death held no more fear. Jesus had pulled its sting!

Jesus knew Mary's name. He knew my name. He knows your name. For him this is personal. He wants us to respond as Mary did. We will never have all of our questions answered. There will be plenty of things we won't understand this side of heaven, but we mustn't let what we don't understand affect what we do understand. Like Mary, we need to take a step of faith and

---

375. Attributed to Voltaire.
376. 1 Corinthians 15:3-8.

worship him.[377] I have watched numbers of people coming to faith in Christ, despite all their unanswered questions. I have watched them have personal encounters with the risen Jesus which have literally changed their lives. A Muslim who recently came to faith, when he was asked what had convinced him to become a Christian, tapped the Bible and said, 'It is this Jesus!'

He is risen

Paul sums up for us the importance of the resurrection. He says if Jesus has not been raised from the dead then our faith is useless and futile and we are still in our sins.[378] Yet this is not the case. Paul announced the verdict over 2,000 years ago when he declared,

> *But in fact, Christ has been raised from the dead. He is the first of a great harvest of all who have died. So you see, just as death came into the world through a man, now the resurrection from the dead has begun through another man. Just as everyone dies because we all belong to Adam, everyone who belongs to Christ will be given new life. But there is an order to this resurrection: Christ was raised as the first of the harvest; then all who belong to Christ will be raised when he comes back.[379]*

On the Thursday night before my father's funeral, I was becoming very anxious. It was just after midnight and Annie

---
377. Matthew 28:9.
378. 1 Corinthians 15:17.
379. 1 Corinthians 15:20-23 [New Living Translation].

and I were quietly talking about the forthcoming funeral and all that had happened in the previous week. Out of nowhere, we started to hear singing. It grew in volume and was clear and beautiful. There were a number of people involved and they were singing a chorus we knew, 'He is Lord.' They sounded as if they were close by, in the house or just outside in the garden. Annie simply sat up in bed listening. I, however, tried to find where the singing was coming from. There was no one in the street. There were no house lights on. In any event, I knew that none of the next-door neighbours had good singing voices! I then went round every room of the house. My mum, my gran and my sister were all fast asleep until I woke them up. I eventually went back to the bedroom. Annie was still listening to the beautiful harmonies. Then suddenly the song drifted away into the night air and all was silent. The peace of God filled the room. I have no natural explanation of what happened or who the singers were. I personally believe God sent angels to comfort us.[380] You may not agree with me. Irrespective of that, what was important was that I was anxious until the peace of God overwhelmed me. The words of the song they were singing were, are and always will be true. They declare his victory and give us hope that goes beyond the grave.

> He is Lord. He is Lord.
> He is risen from the dead
> And he is Lord.
> Every knee shall bow,
> Every tongue confess
> That Jesus Christ is Lord!

---

380. Hebrews 1:14.

THROUGH

'He Has Risen'

CHAPTER 10

THE SHADOW OF THE CROSS

'Into his Presence'

About 150 years ago, William Holman Hunt painted a number of pictures of Jesus. One of his lesser-known works is, rather unsettlingly, called *The Shadow of Death*. The picture shows Jesus working as a carpenter. Hunt painted him looking towards the sun and stretching out his arms. Behind him the shadow of his outstretched arms falls on to a wooden beam which is holding his tools. His shadow looks as if it is on a cross. Holman Hunt's point is that Jesus lived his short life on earth in the shadow of the cross. The Gospel writers tell us that Jesus lived knowing what was going to happen to him[381] and never once sought to avoid his destiny. No one ever lived like Jesus. No one ever died like Jesus. He lived well. He died well.

As Jesus hung on the cross he reconciled man to God. He himself bridged the great divide caused by our sin. Yet, as he hung between heaven and earth, his arms were stretched out wide for us. Jesus reaches out to any who will come to him. He doesn't care where we come from. He's not bothered about our family background, our life experiences, our educational achievements, our sphere of influence or how much disposable income we have. Through his death and resurrection he brings sinful men and women to God and creates a new community. At the foot of the cross there is room for all who will humble themselves and receive by faith what Jesus has won for them.

We all live in the shadow of the cross – whether we like it or not. All of us will have to stand before God. We will have to give an account of what we did with the life he gave us.[382] We can do no better than learn from Jesus. The challenge for us is to live well and die well in the light of all that Jesus has accomplished.

---

381. Mark 8:31, 32.
382. Hebrews 9:27.

Living well

The shadow thrown by the cross is the gospel. Paul encourages each one of us, 'Whatever happens, conduct yourselves in a manner worthy of the gospel of Christ.'[383] So what does this way of living 'look like'?

It means loving God with all our heart, mind and strength.[384] Intimacy with God really is possible. Each of us can know him as our Father because Jesus' death has opened the way into God's presence. Amazingly, we can know forgiveness, whatever we have done. We can receive grace and mercy, despite how we have behaved. God's Spirit will dwell within us and quench our thirst for intimacy with God. If we live in the shadow of the cross, worship will mark our lives. We will be a thankful, appreciative and worshipping people wherever we are: on our own, at home or at work. Our goal will be simply to live in a way that pleases him.[385]

Living like this must affect our relationships. Our aim must be to love people because God loves people.[386] We should be passionate to share the gospel with any who will listen. Our relationships are to be marked by selflessness. We must put others' needs first. There should be a deep sense of togetherness because through Jesus we are committed to one another. We are to be kind when others don't deserve it. Forgiveness should be freely given, not bartered for. This is necessary because not one of us is perfect. We, of all people, know what it is to be forgiven by God when we did nothing

---

383. Philippians 1:27.
384. Matthew 22:37.
385. 2 Corinthians 5:9.
386. John 3:16.

to deserve it. Living in the shadow of the cross means loving God's people. Paul sums up this way of living: 'I have been crucified with Christ and I no longer live, but Christ lives in me. The life I live in the body, I live by faith in the Son of God, who loved me and gave himself for me.'[387]

Is this really possible? Yes, but only if Jesus remains at the centre of our lives. We need the ongoing help of the Holy Spirit who enables us to believe in Christ.[388] We will never please God on our own by doing better or working harder. I know, because I foolishly keep trying. It never works. Time after time I find my Father drawing me back to the foot of the cross where I realise once again I can only please him by receiving his free gift of grace. I need to be filled continually with his Spirit and then allow him to lead me.[389] The fruit of this kind of life is evident to everyone. Love, joy, peace, patience, kindness, goodness, faithfulness, gentleness and self-control are the marks of Christ. No wonder Paul says that, if we want to live by the Spirit, we must keep in step with the Spirit. At one level it is an impossible task but with God helping us all things are possible.

Whatever happens in life, whether good or bad, nothing compares to the wonder of knowing Jesus. He is worth it. I don't know about you, but my struggles in life start as soon as I lose sight of him. If only I looked to him more quickly . . . The longer I dwell under the shadow of the cross the more I want to fix my eyes on Jesus, the author of my faith.[390]

---

387. Galatians 2:20.
388. Galatians 3:1-3.
389. Galatians 5:16-26.
390. Hebrews 12:2.

Dying well

Death is not a popular pastime. No one likes being reminded of their own mortality. Most people try to avoid thinking about it in the bizarre hope that it will go away. Yet one day it will be too late. Whether we like it or not, none of us can avoid having to cross what is the final frontier. It is far better that we come and stand in the light of all that Jesus has done for us. If we do, we can die well knowing that eternity with our Father is certain.

On that day the Apostle John says of everyone who has put their personal faith in Jesus: 'They will see his face'.[391]

Nonetheless, grief and loss are real. We must never sweep them under the carpet. In 1991 a good friend was killed in a car accident. He was a committed Christian, yet for many of us it was a very sad time. He was only in his early twenties. I remember immediately after the funeral service someone saying, 'I don't know why everyone is upset, he's gone to glory!' The author and church leader Phil Moore observes that people who say such things are being cruel, even if their intentions are good.[392] It is right and proper for us to grieve the passing of fellow believers, even though we know they have gone to a better place.

In the book of Acts we read of one of the leaders of the early Church being martyred.[393] Luke, who wrote Acts, tells us that Stephen robustly defended the gospel. The crowd's response was to stone him. At the last, he lifted his eyes to heaven and saw Jesus standing at the right hand of God. Then he committed his spirit into Jesus' hands. It sounds familiar, doesn't it!

---
391. Revelation 22:4.
392. Phil Moore, *Straight to the Heart of Acts* (Monarch Books, 2010), p.92.
393. Acts 6:8–7:60.

After this, are we then told his friends threw a party because he had gone to a better place? No, we are not! Luke says: 'Godly men buried Stephen and mourned deeply for him.'[394] These friends were confident about where Stephen had gone. They knew his body was just a shell. They were certain that death was not the end. For them there was a huge personal risk involved in publicly being associated with Stephen, even though he was dead. Yet these men took his broken, battered body and buried it. The language Luke uses implies that they were godly as they beat their chests in deep grief over Stephen's death.[395] Jesus was himself indignant about death when his friend Lazarus died.[396] The Bible tells us that the death of believers is precious to God.[397] We are not to grieve as those with no hope[398] but we are to grieve nonetheless. Grief is a godly response. The Bible encourages us with laments. In our grief, we worship God. We remember the person. We remember especially how their life has enriched us and shown us something of Christ that we might not otherwise have seen. And in it all we remember Jesus raised from the dead. This is our gospel.[399] Those left behind should honour those who have lived well and died well.

A quick word about Stephen himself. We are told that he was full of the Holy Spirit and God's grace.[400] He died well. Death held no fear for him. He was certain of his future. He held firmly to his faith. He looked to Christ to the end.

Heaven was opened. Jesus was waiting. Stephen saw him.

---

394. Acts 8:2.
395. Phil Moore, *Straight to the Heart of Acts*, p.92.
396. John 11:38-43. The Greek word for 'deeply moved' in v.38 is 'enbrimaomai' and it would also have been used of a warhorse snorting in readiness for battle.
397. Psalm 116:15.
398. 1 Thessalonians 4:13.
399. 2 Timothy 2:8.
400. Acts 6:8, 10.

One of my first jobs involved working in the Afan Valley near Port Talbot. It was known locally as 'Little Switzerland' although I'm not sure the Swiss Tourist Board was ever made aware of the comparison. Part way up the Afan Valley is the small community of Cymmer, with a population of just a few thousand people. Cymmer holds a place in my heart but not for any reason you might expect.

When I was 23 years old, God broke into my messed-up life. My best friend Adrian's father, Gareth, encouraged both of us to wholeheartedly pursue God. He shared how God had used him when he was our age. His story still inspires me. As a newly qualified teacher he'd got his first job at the secondary school in Cymmer. As he was the new teacher, the Head gave him the 'privilege' of teaching the difficult class of older teenage boys that no one else wanted, on a Friday afternoon. He was given free rein with the lesson. He was a Christian and so he planned to share with them about Jesus. To say it didn't go well the first week would be an understatement. The boys were badly behaved and unresponsive. Gareth was discouraged and disheartened. An old lady in a small local church at a midweek prayer meeting encouraged Gareth that he shouldn't give up and that God was with him. The following Friday afternoon he started again. This time everything was different. The boys all listened. I remember him saying you could have heard a pin drop as he shared what Jesus had done on the cross for them. All of the boys in the class, about 30 of them, gave their lives to Christ that day, many of them in tears. In the following weeks they started meeting outside school so that friends, girlfriends and family could join with them. A considerable number of people became followers of Christ.

One of the boys who had come to faith became seriously ill and was not given long to live. Gareth went to visit him in hospital. As he entered the hospital room the boy was lying in bed. His face was visible on the pillow but his eyes were closed. He had slipped into a coma. His mother was at the bedside. She was understandably grief-stricken and also angry with God. Gareth bore the brunt of her anger. 'Look at my boy . . . where's your God now?' she vented her frustration. As she was doing this, her son's eyes opened and quietly he said, 'Mam, mam . . . don't say that . . .' The room went silent . . .

Looking beyond her, he whispered, 'Can you see him, mam? Can you see him?'

Then he closed his eyes and passed into the presence of the Lord.

One day we will face the inevitable final challenge that death poses. In that moment there will only be one question that matters . . .

Can you see him?

APPENDIX

40 DAYS THROUGH LENT

For each of the next 40 days read the excerpt for that day and then take time to meditate on what you have read. This season provokes us to examine our own heart and draw near to God in prayer.

Day	Section to read	Page(s)
1	The unexpected silence*	20-23
2	The unusual script	23-25
3	The innocent sufferer	25-27
4	The perfect substitute	27-29
5	The acceptable sacrifice	29-30
6	Threads of the tapestry and proof of victory	30-32
7	Then there is Jesus*	34-36
8	An act of significance	36-37
9	A place of significance	37-41
10	Words of significance (1) 'Father'	41-43
11	Words of significance (2) 'Forgive them'	43-46
12	Words of significance (3) 'For they know not what they do'	47-49
13	Lasting significance	49-50
14	The ridicule*	52-56
15	The rebuke	56-59
16	The request	59-61
17	The response and the result	62-64
18	Created for community*	66-69
19	Crushing of community	70-71

20	Conceiving a new community	71-73
21	The challenge of this new community	73-75
22	Cross-shaped community	75-80
23	Lost intimacy and persevering faith	82-85
24	A rhetorical question . . .	86-89
25	God-forsaken	89-92
26	Certain outcome	93-94
27	His provision and his test*	96-99
28	His humanity and his longing	100-104
29	His offer – are we thirsty?	104-109
30	Suffering ceased*	112-115
31	Prophecy fulfilled	115-116
32	Satan defeated	116-117
33	Sin atoned for	118-119
34	Law satisfied	119-120
35	Redemption secured	121-122
36	Relationship restored – job done!	122-124
37	God shows his hand* and takes matters into his own hands	126-131
38	Jesus is in good hands	131-134
39	Getting it at first hand	135-136
40	In safe hands	136-138

*including introduction